# aoe

Exploring possibilities:
A journey of architectural fantasy

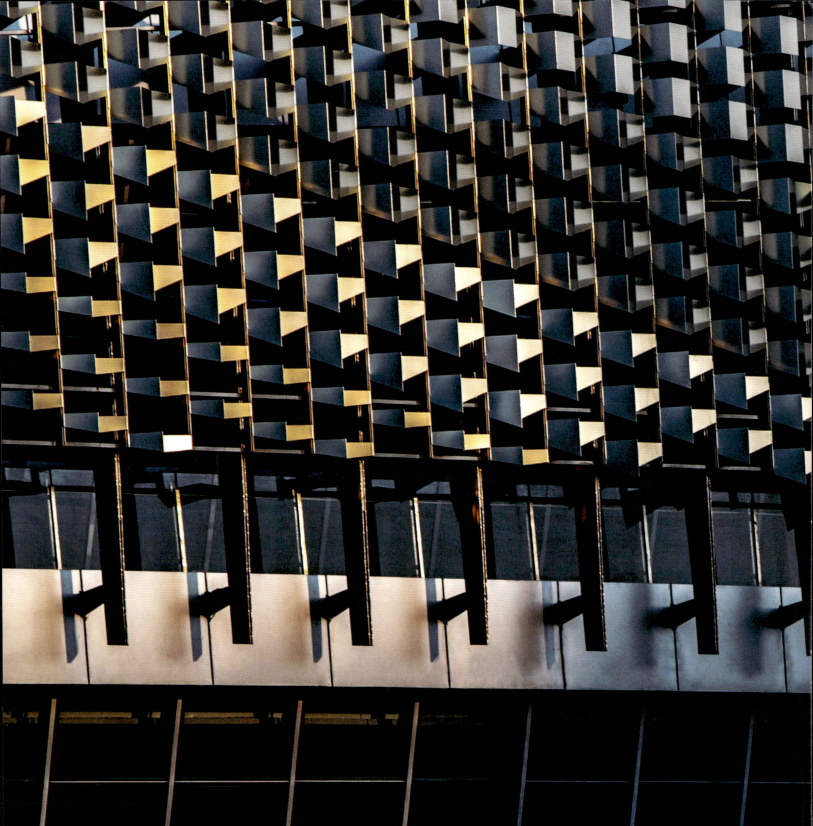

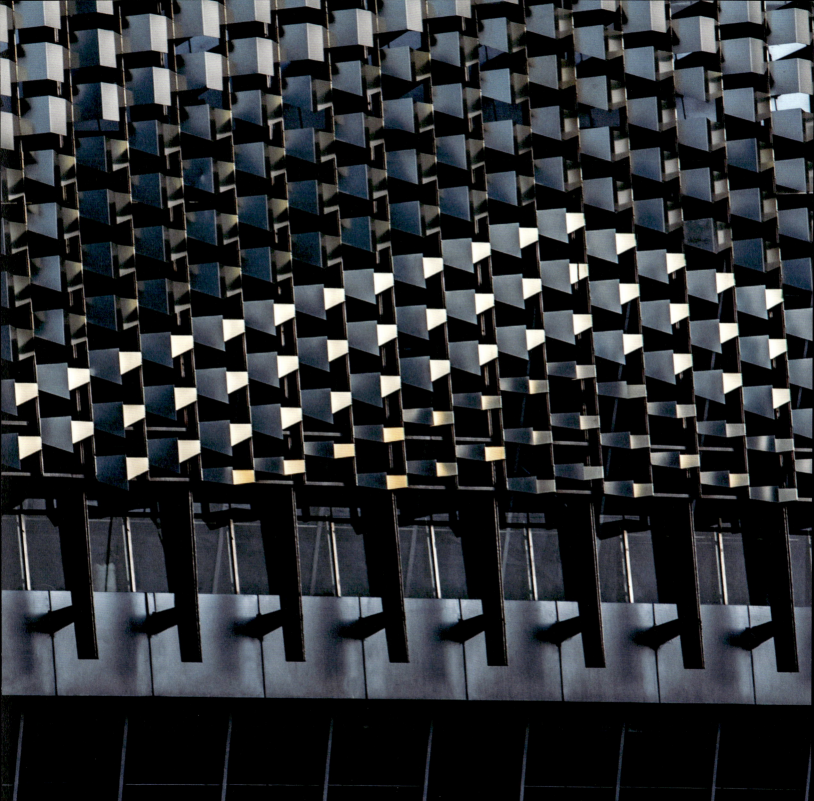

# aoe

**Exploring possibilities:
A journey of architectural fantasy**

Foreword by Na Risi
Interview by James McCown
Epilogue by Qun Wen
Edited by Oscar Riera Ojeda

OSCAR RIERA OJEDA
PUBLISHERS

# contents

**010** —— Foreword by Na Risi

**014** —— Interview with Qun Wen by James McCown

**022** —— Selected Works:
024 —— Chongqing Sunac One Central Mansion Sales Pavillion
052 —— ShuiFa Info Town Property Exhibition Center
084 —— One Sino Park
108 —— Shanxiao Sales Pavilion
134 —— Sino-Italian Culture Exchange City Reception Center
164 —— Sino-Italian Culture Exchange City Reception Center - The Chinese Cultural Hall
202 —— Courtyard No. 1 Heze
226 —— Haikou International Duty Free Reception Center
254 —— Heze Nanjing Road Sales Office
274 —— Yongjiang Reception Center

**292** —— Epilogue by Qun Wen

**298** —— Firm Profile

**304** —— Book Credits

# foreword

by
Na Risi

"Without events, there is no architecture", this was the core concept Qun Wen had in mind when he founded aoe in 2016.

In 2016, China's architectural design found itself at a crossroads: following nearly 40 years of rapid development that caught the imagination of the world, China's urban construction experienced a downturn. Its architectural design shifted away from the influence of the west and shoddily built mass developments while, as the economy slowed down, the scene began to stagnate and people began to reflect on the issues raised by decades of fast-paced development. How should architectural design deal with environmental issues and culture? Localization and globalization? Urban and rural dynamics? Local materials and industrial products? Traditional craftsmanship and modern production? The answers to these dilemmas have shaped the thinking of Chinese architectural design after the development boom and in the post-recession period to come it will be essential for Chinese design to draw on the latest ideas from the West but also to pay more attention to the relationship between people and the environment, to the survival and development of local cultures buffeted by global trends, the connotations and scope of the constructions themselves, and to place architectural design within a broader logic.

This period was not a good time to enter the market: the slowdown that followed the boom saw many design companies struggling to survive. The only ones who did were those capable of truly facing up to the issue, solving problems and finding a way to sustainably develop their business, thus allowing them to weather the storm of the recession and even to thrive.

aoe was created in such a context.

aoe's core design concept, which deliberately avoided grand narratives, offered a more natural, sensual, rational and subtly balanced approach to architectural design, an approach that was closer to the essence of design and construction. This concept ensured that the company's design is more concerned with the relationship between people and architecture, people and space, people and things, the environment, space, materials, and structure, and the internal logic of technology, eschewing lavish, meaningless decoration and formalism so that its architecture establishes deep roots and foundations, becomes a part of the environment and makes a positive contribution to it.

This effortless approach to design may come from Wen's educational background and work experience. Wen studied at the Xi'an University of Architecture and Technology, which has the most free and open atmosphere of the top eight architecture universities in China, before obtaining a Master of Architecture from Cal Poly Pomona in California. Wen then worked for an extensive period (over ten years) at HMC, WOODS BAGOT, RMJM,

AEDAS, AECOM, UAD and other international architectural design firms, accumulating a wealth of experience and knowledge in different fields. This educational background and professional experience allowed Wen to develop an approach that implements logical principles of architectural design that take into account both extensive globalization and the human scale, as well as a willingness to cherish local distinctions. This is an architecture that focuses on specific events, establishing a holistic philosophical approach to design that takes the event as its point of departure and carefully analyzes and organizes the different factors involved to deduce the logical form and so implement a plan for each building. This means that aoe is not only founded in a unified chain of values but also the deductive logic of event → factor → form, making the building a unique location that blends seamlessly with its environment, whether through the "symbiosis between human and nature" of the One Sino Park, "learning from the land" as seen in Shanxiao, the "Bright Moon Clear Spring" of the ShuiFa Info Town Property Exhibition Center, the "Ancient and Modern Periods of China and the West" of the Sino-Italian Culture Exchange City Reception Center, or the "deconstruction and reorganization release" of the Haikou International Duty Free Reception Center. All these projects vividly and brilliantly embody the design philosophy of "think global, work local".

In the contemporary world, when humanity is swamped with information, it is vitally important that we emphasize our interactions with one another. Architectural design must organize people's residential, work and leisure spaces so that they fully acknowledge and encourage this interaction. In addition to this functional and constructional logic, aoe's designs take into account nature, the humanities, art, technology, materials and craftsmanship, ensuring that the architectural space has multiple connotations and an enhanced cultural purpose.

Architecture inevitably intervenes within a larger natural environment, composing cities as human social spaces; it cannot exist in isolation from that environment. aoe's architectural design firmly grasps the context of the environment and the city, making it a continuation of the environment, the city and the context with the goal of making worthwhile contributions to their rhythms and cycles.

Since its inception, aoe has become a major design institution in China, its international organizational structure and excellent working reputation have increasingly attracted attention and praise at home and abroad, with the studio's built works winning a number of domestic and international awards. The future looks bright and exciting and there are surely many brilliant projects to come.

Wen and I were classmates in college, and we have been in constant contact and profound dialogue since then, so it was a pleasure to write the preface for this book.

*Na Risi. Mi Zhai, March 12, 2022.*

# interview

with
Qun Wen
by
James McCown

Q&A Session Between Qun Wen and James McCown
January 11, 2022

**James McCown: Mr. Wen, thank you for taking the time to speak with me. Please talk to me about your background – your hometown, your education.**

Qun Wen: My hometown, Xi'an, is a very historic city. That had a real influence on me. It's where they found the underground Terra Cotta Warriors in 1974. I got my undergraduate training in architecture in China and got my master's in the United States, at California Polytechnic Pomona.

I have very deep roots in Chinese culture. Often the client has a very strong and clear idea of some kind of a Chinese style or Chinese architecture. So yes, that's why some of my works, you can see the influence of Chinese architecture. But it's not just a copy of the like a traditional Chinese architecture, but a way of developing it with a new interpretation. And with new technology and the new materials, we develop; we don't just copy.

Most of the classic Chinese buildings look in some way like ancient paintings by Chinese artists. You always see some trees or landscapes surrounding the buildings. Right. So you see the architecture and the people and the environment as a whole, as one part. Yes, that's a Chinese philosophy.

**JM: In the past you've often talked about the intersection of culture, commerce and architecture.**

QW: Our office and work has always been related to culture and commerce.

**JM: Is it the responsibility of a real estate developer to be a patron of good architecture?**

QW: Yes. The last ten years have been amazing in terms of the buildings built. But now things are changing – the market is cooling. There's more opportunity to sit down and talk to the real estate client about commerce and design.

**JM: Let's talk about architecture and the public realm**

QW: Our library in Korea is very much in the public realm. It's open to all and we created spaces where people can gather. Since it's close to an airport, we created an outdoor gathering area where you can watch the planes take off.

**JM: The reception building at Haikou – is it a reception center?**

QW: Yes it's a reception center for a very high-end shopping mall that the developers are building.

**JM: Talk to me about the Wan Zhou City Reception Center, with the dramatic bridge.**

QW: It's a function of a spectacular cliff site. If you look at the building, it's part of the landscape. We had the idea of making the building more integrated into nature. It's a reception center now for selling the apartments. But later it will revert into a community center for the complex.

**JM: I'm very interested in the Chengdu Olympic Planning Exhibition Hall. Its upward curves, are they inspired by classic Chinese architecture with its upward curving eaves?**

QW: Yes.

**JM: It seems to be very much formed by circular geometry. The late Wolf von Eckardt, the Washington Post architecture critic, called such architecture "Capricious forms based and merciless logic." Talk to me about that project, if you could, and how the geometry was formed, how the idea formed in your head.**

QW: Well, the building is located on a very special site on a peninsula, so the site is very linear. That's why we developed an oval shape. Another main idea of this project is trying to develop an architecture that grows from that landscape. It's a sloped path so people can easily go to the rooftop at different levels. The roof is in effect a pathway – it becomes a 3D trail. People can follow the curve and go all the way to the top. Actually that's the main idea because the building has a very strong theme, which is the power and unity of the Olympics. We tried to develop an idea of people taking a trail and going up to the rooftop. That's the main concept of the project.

**JM: Courtyard No. 1 in Heze – this doesn't seem inspired by anything in particular. Speak to me about that project.**

QW: The building is a transparent glass box. We tried to make this a venue for the entire city. Inside the glass box is very dynamic coloring which draws people in.

**JM: A reception center for developers – that seems to be a theme in your work.**

QW: Yes, we wanted to give people of sense of what their future life will be. It's about selling apartments and it showcases their future lifestyle.

**JM: Let's discuss the Shanxiao Sales Office.**

QW: We tried to give a Chinese flavor to the building. The louvers are both aesthetic and functional. The clouds in the mountains in the city were the inspiration for the louvers.

**JM: Chongqing Sunac One Central Mansion Sales Office – it has a very ethereal, dreamlike feel to it. Explain this building please.**

QW: The building is now a sales office but it will be converted into a kindergarten. The metal mesh on the exterior is a special addition – the building works really well. This mesh curtain will be removed before it reverts to being a kindergarten.

**JM: The reflecting pond also seems to be a theme I see again and again.**

QW: Yes, this allows the building to be reflected and gives it a very tranquil feeling. It's always inspired by nature – there are always angles in nature.

**JM: Guilong Port Sales Office in Guiyang – here's another sales office.**

QW: The developer wants to turn it from a sales center into something else. He likes the way it turned out. There is a courtyard at the center of the building. This is a very typical Chinese gesture. And the curved roof is inspired by traditional Chinese architecture with the upturned eaves.

**JM: The Liuzhou Ice and Snow Exhibition Center – was that built for the Olympics?**

QW: No. It's a theme park which has a very large ski ramp. It's a theme park for skiing and skating. It's a tropical city and they never have snow. So the developer wanted the citizens to be able to enjoy winter sports. It also has retail streets with stores and restaurants.

**JM: Can you delve more into the influence of classical Chinese architecture?**

QW: Traditional Chinese architecture has a very strong influence on our office's work. It's a system. It's not just a form. It's a system that responds to nature. It has a very methodical function. It's very complicated but every single element has its function. It's all very logical. If you look at our buildings, they are all the result of serious study…they don't have a "style."

**JM: Are you satisfied with your body of work at this stage? Is there a project type you'd like to do like an airport or a hospital?**

QW: Over the past five years we've had a lot of buildings completed. But I'd like to do an airport or a hospital. Buildings that have a large impact on the city and the public realm.

**JM: It seems to me that many of your buildings evoke the designs of 20th century form givers like Moshe Safdie and Oscar Niemeyer. Your forms are at once capricious but also grounded in a very rational basis formed by rigorous and precise manipulation of geometry. Please talk to me about that.**

QW: Yes, actually, I think you're right. If you look at all the projects, geometry actually is a very important part of them. I believe that geometry is a way to know the human condition, a way to understand the world.

**JM: Talk about other architects who have influenced you.**

QW: Maybe not only Moshe Safdie and Oscar Niemeyer. I like architects like Rem Koolhaas, Thom Mayne of Morphosis and Frank Gehry. You can see some influence of these architects in my work.

**JM: When I look at the Songdo Library in Korea, at first I notice a roof garden. Then I'm also interested in in the fact that it almost appears to float, weightless. It reminds me of Niemeyer's Museum in Niteroi, near Rio de Janeiro. It has a very light appearance to it.**

QW: Both buildings are cantilevered with new technology. Architecture is always about dealing with the gravity. That's the essence of architecture.

Then there's the circular shape of the library. Actually, we did a lot of studies and there were many schemes, some of which were not circular in shape but more rectangular. On the east side of this building, there's a residential community. That's why we developed a rounded shape to minimize the impact of the building on the surrounding residents.

Also, if you look at the building, it's actually tilting, right? Yes, because we did a very careful study to minimize direct sunlight and heat gain in the summer while maximizing heat gain in the winter. So actually, there are some sustainable concerns in this design. It was designed for sustainable reasons and not just for the look of the building.

**JM: I often see your work referred to as "ethereal," and that's an interesting word because it suggests a sense of being "otherworldly" or "too beautiful to be true." The Information Exhibition Center at Jinan Shandong project certainly meets that criterion. Its glass is light and seemingly evaporates into the surrounding sky. Steven Holl has done a**

lot of work with glass here in the U.S., as has Frank Gehry with his IAC building on the West Side of Manhattan. Talk to me about the very lightness that you achieve in that project and how you arrived at that idea.**

QW: Well, when we started the Exhibition Center we studied the site and we noticed it was in a very remote area in the city of Jinan. The quality of the surroundings was not very good. Yes. This is a concern because this project is a building for the client to sell its properties. The building was next to a construction site, which was not very pleasant. So we decided to wrap the building with a layer of the perforated aluminum panels.

**JM: With this building we have cubes that are basically tilted. Why is that?**

QW: Well, it represents the rocks there. It's developed based on an ancient Chinese point. It says something about rocks and the landscapes. I don't know how to say it in English, but it's like a Bonsai tree. You know, with the rocks on the side.

**JM: One Sino Park – it doesn't seem as influenced by Chinese architecture as by the American firms like Frank Gehry and Morphosis. Talk to me about that.**

QW: The building, too, is located on a cliff. It has a unique and special site. Chongqing is a huge and dynamic city and we tried to express this dynamism. I was studying in the United States at Cal Poly Pomona. Being in greater Los Angeles, I definitely came under the influence of architects like Gehry and Thom Mayne of Morphosis. When I started this project, the construction on the site was almost finished. The client already had started filling their offices and then for some reason they stopped and decided to change the design. So I started from there. The building is located on a very special site and on the east side and there is a very clear, steep cliff and on the west side a main citadel. So we put a very solid wall on the west side. Also, to keep the building very artistic in feel like a museum, on the west side we put a series of fragmented panels. There is going to be a park there in the future, so we provided opportunities for people to overlook the surrounding cliffs.

**JM: I must say that I don't quite know what to make of the Sino-Italian Culture Exchange City Reception Center in Chengdu. It evokes Roman architecture. This seems very postmodernism right out of the 1980s. Please discuss this building and especially how it is influenced by Roman architecture.**

QW: This was actually a governmental project. It was commissioned to have a very strong theme. It is a collaboration between the Chengdu government and the Italian government. Actually, you can see some of the

ancient Roman architecture elements, right? Some of them are required by the client. I mean, they wanted to see a very strong image for people to understand Italian architecture.

**JM: And it was about celebrating the economic connection between an Italy and China, right?**

QW: Yes, exactly. The building shows the intersection of the Chinese and Italian cultures. So at the beginning, we didn't have these elements. We developed a very contemporary building with the bow forms. But after several rounds talking to the client, they wanted us to put all those elements in the building. So that's why you see Roman architectural elements in the building.

**JM: But you say the client wanted an evocation of Italian architecture and then you have maybe the Asian influence with the curved walls. So it combines the two cultures, right?**

QW: Right. The curve was again back to the geometry of architecture. And also it creates the shadows, and it feels like the building has, how do you say it, a very strong image as an independent object in the environment.

**JM: Tell me how you work when you have ideas. Do you sketch out your ideas or do you have your staff make models of your ideas, or both?**

QW: I do a lot of sketches on my iPad. I did a calculation last year, 2021. I made around 1,500 sketches. Yeah, I do that every day. You know, I develop the concept, I do revisions, I do a lot of things on the iPad.

**JM: Then you have your staff make models of the most compelling ideas?**

QW: Right, yes.

**JM: Well, I'm asking because I'm very interested in how you arrive at your forms and contexts. I'm trying to get at your creative process. Is it a process of sketching? Is it a process of creating models? How do you arrive at your forms?**

QW: I think with the sketches. It's a very important tool to develop the ideas. Yes, there are a lot of sketches and as you'll notice our office doesn't have a clear identifiable style. There are many different approaches.

**JM: So the office does not have a signature style?**

QW: No, no. I don't like the idea of having the same style and developing

ideas at different sites, and so that's why we actually focus on the core ideas of the project, not just the form. It's all about the building and space and the users, and their relationship to each other. In our buildings the form is probably the result of investigations, not the first thing we think about. It's all about very rational logic. After a series of studies, we develop the solutions and come up with a form.

**JM: I see. Let's talk about geography. Most of your work is in China and Korea. And yet you studied in the United States. Do you have a desire to design in America and Europe or do you tend to remain focused on Asia?**

QW: Yes, of course, I would like to expand our geographic reach. If there's some opportunities, if we could do some work in the States or in Europe, that would be great.

**JM: You've been widely published by the magazines and the architecture websites. Has that helped you? Do you get inquiries from Europe and the United States about possible projects? Or do you have someone who does outreach to look for potential projects there? Talk to me about expanding the geographic range of your work.**

QW: So far, not from the States or Europe, but recently we got an email from Russia. Very interesting. They are trying to do a high-end residential project in Moscow. And yet we don't know yet. We've set up a meeting for this afternoon.

**JM: What was the effect of studying in the U.S., given that you were a student during very interesting and changing times in architecture? Please reflect on that for me.**

QW: Well, studying at Cal Poly definitely had a very big, big impact on my career. You know, the education systems in China and the States are so different.

**JM: How so?**

QW: In China, the student follows the instructions of the professor. Whether you change your projects or not, it's all about the instructor. But in the States, the student has it different. They're free to develop their own ideas. They can challenge the instructor. That's a very, very big difference.

**JM: Who are your own personal architectural heroes?**

QW: Well, I like a lot of architects. The name of the company, aoe, architecture of event, came from the expression by Bernard Tschumi. He's a very good, a great architect. And the theory developed by Tschumi has had a very strong influence: "Without event, without activity, without function, architecture must be thought of as the combination of spaces, events and movements, without precedence or hierarchy between these terms." Yes!

**JM: Where do you see aoe 10 years from now?**

QW: Well, to be honest I have no idea. And I don't set up goals. I just follow the natural path of my career. Right. I do hope our office can be more exposed to the world internationally and that we can get projects in Europe, in America and in different parts of the world.

**JM: Is there any particular building type that you prefer? Is it an educational facility or a public facility versus a private developer? Talk to me about the project type that you like to design the most.**

QW: Well, I that's really a good question. I'm interested in doing projects that can serve our communities. You know, public users. Because you can see a lot of my works are like a sales office. They're private. So it's not really a building for the public. Right. I really want to do something to make a bigger contribution to the society, to the neighborhood.

**JM: The public realm, we call it here in the U.S.**

QW: Yes

**JM: Reflect on collaborating with landscape architects. How does that process go in China? I'm not familiar with whether there are independent landscape architects. Are they folded into architecture firms and how do you work with them to make a beautiful landscape for your buildings?**

QW: Well, yes, we in China, we do have independent landscape architects and we work with landscape architects a lot. Sometimes when we start a project, we start from the planning of the project working with a land-scape architect early on. We can start from there and we discuss how we can communicate right to make the landscape work with the buildings. Same thing with interior designers.

**JM: Exactly. Now, by the same token, how do you work with structural engineers because many of your buildings are cantilevered and so boldly conceived? How do you work with them?**

QW: Well, yes (laughing) we create a lot of problems and headaches for structural engineers. But when we're working with them we don't just tell them, "Hey, this is what we want." We collaborate with them. We find different solutions. Sometimes we come to a compromise. Right? For example, if this structural engineer says, "Oh, this can be very subtle; we can study if we make this cantilever smaller." It's a process of negotiation and communication.

**JM: Well, do you have any closing thoughts for me? Feel free to talk to me about things that are important to you. Give me some closing thoughts about your philosophy and your passions.**

QW: Architecture is a very difficult profession. You have to coordinate a lot of different things. It's not just about the design concepts of this country, it's about how you use the different resources to make the building real. For me, the architecture is not really defined by architects. It's defined by the needs of the users and the compelling issues of the site. The architectural answer is pretty much already there, it's just a question of finding it. Architecture is the place at go to find solutions. It's all about a solution-oriented methodology. Yes. Understanding.

**JM: Absolutely. That's a very good way to end. Thank you so much for your time.**

QW: Thank you.

James Moore McCown is a Boston-based architectural journalist who writes for numerous design publications including *Metropolis, Architect's Newspaper* and *AD PRO Architectural Digest.* He has collaborated with Oscar Riera Ojeda on several books including the *Architecture in Detail* series which comprised four volumes: *Elements, Materials, Colors and Spaces.* McCown studied journalism at Loyola University New Orleans and holds an ALM (Master's Degree) in the history of art and architecture from Harvard University, where his thesis on modern Brazilian architecture received an Honorable Mention, Dean's Award, Best ALM Thesis (2007). He lives in Newton, Massachusetts.

# selected

works

Chongqing Sunac One Central Mansion Sales Pavillion

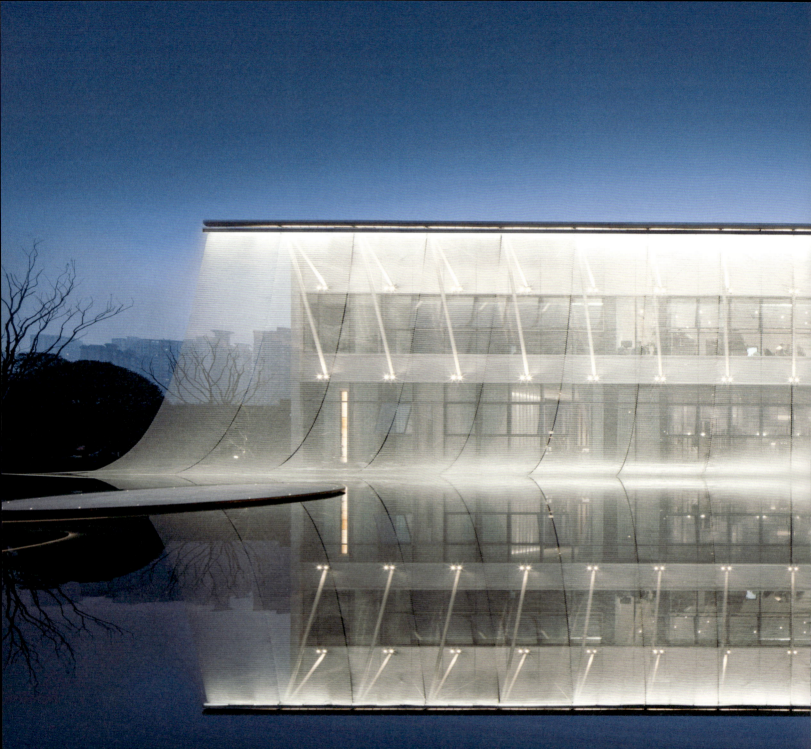

**Project Name** Chongqing Sunac One Central Mansion Sales Pavillion
**Architecture Firm** aoe
**Architect in Charge** Qun Wen
**Design Team** Yibo Wang, Chao Xie, Yusong Zhang
**Completion Year** 2017
**Built Area** 2,000 m²
**Project Location** Chongqing, China

We are trying to find a way to engage new technology, materials, ideas to excavate the essence of Chinese architectural culture, to create a new form of Chinese architecture adapting to the developments of the modern era, to return the value of Chinese culture. We hope to use design to regain the essence of Chinese culture and reshape our cultural self-confidence.

Sunac as one of the largest developers in China will develop a luxury apartment project in Chongqing located on Huxie Road. We are committed to design their sales office. Based on the regulations, the sales office will be converted into a kindergarten after its use as a sales office. The difficulty of the project is that two different functions have completely different requirements for space, form and appearance. The strategy we adopted is to add another layer of removable green skin, the metal mesh, outside the building for sustainable and imagery purpose. This layer of skin creates a unique façade of the sales office which is conveyed by the core concept of Chinese architecture from the artistic conception of the expression. Different from the western architecture which is based on a stone masonry construction system, ancient Chinese architecture does not use geometric form as the basis of architectural performance, on the contrary, in the Chinese-style wood structure, the emphasis is more on the expression of architectural logic following the natural law. Structural components such as pillars, beams, brackets, rafters, Purlin and so on are all exposed, all comply with the natural mechanics of the law, so it will appear without affectation, especially the roof of the arc. The overhangs of the eaves form the gray space and it creates a vague zone merging the nature and building into one to achieve the symbiotic state of man and nature.

The concept of the sales office is in the inheritance of such a concept. The use of metal fabric as the secondary skin forms a sustainable curtain to protect the building from direct sunlight for energy saving. Also the internal and external spaces are linked visually and spatially in an elegant transition. Translucent materials presented by the looming visual blur convey a rich level of the depth in space. At the same time, the graceful arc of metal fabric formed by natural mechanical logic salutes the Chinese architecture which conforms to the logic of natural structure. The elegant modern steel structure is exposed. The translucency together with elegant landscape creates a poetic zen space. Although the architectural form and the material are modern, the core idea is the same as Chinese architectural philosophy. The Tao Nature, formless is the ultimate sophistication.

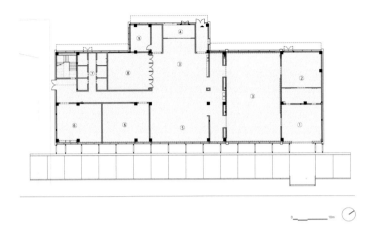

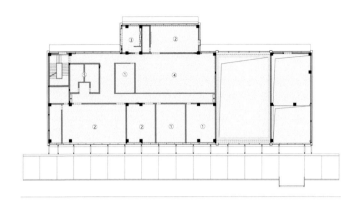

ground floor plan / sales office

01 reception
02 video room
03 model area
04 bar
05 discussion area
06 vip room
07 restroom
08 multifunctional room
09 office

second floor plan / sales office

01 reception
02 meeting room
03 locker
04 work area
05 restroom

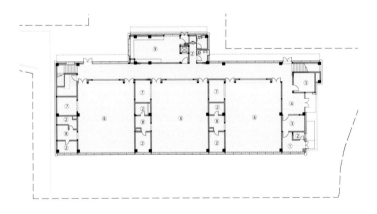

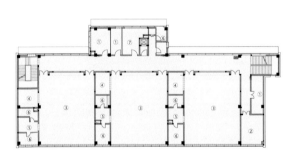

ground floor plan / kindergarten

01 observation room
02 restroom
03 checking room
04 lobby
05 security room
06 activity/sleeping area
07 locker room
08 washroom
09 kitchen

second floor plan

01 office
02 meeting room
03 activity/sleeping area
04 locker room
05 washroom
06 restroom
07 storage

selected works ———— 029

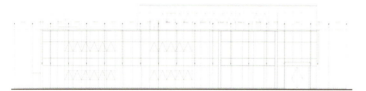

elevation

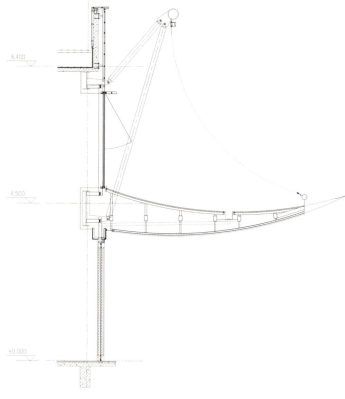

entrance detail

selected works — 041

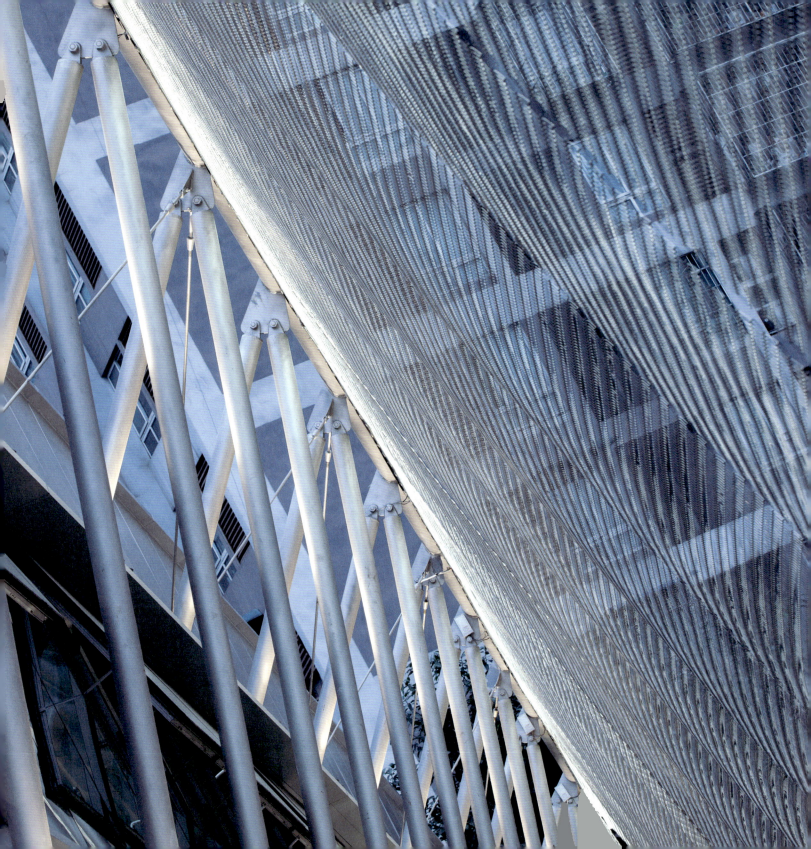

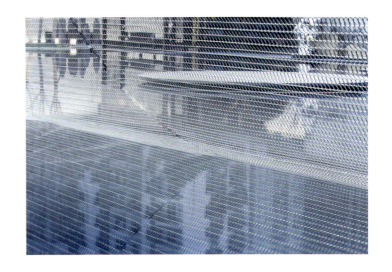

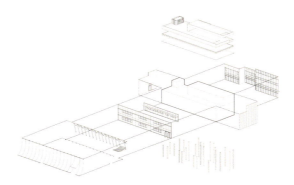

exploded axonometric

selected works — 045

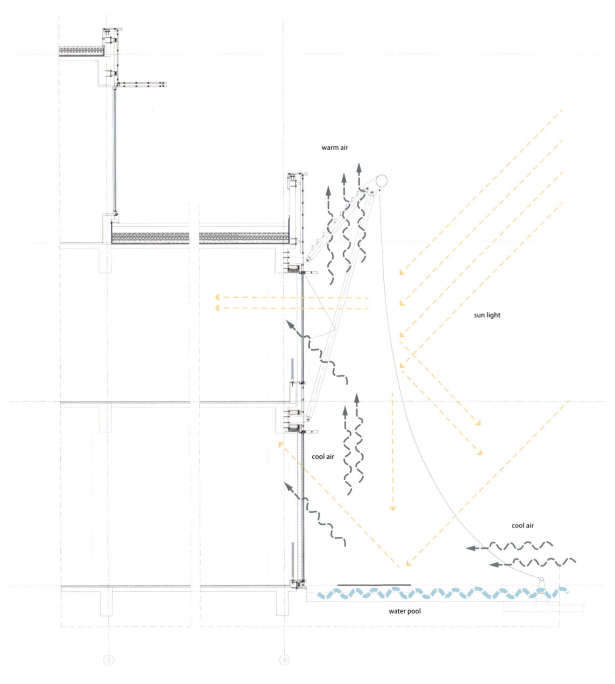

section and analysis

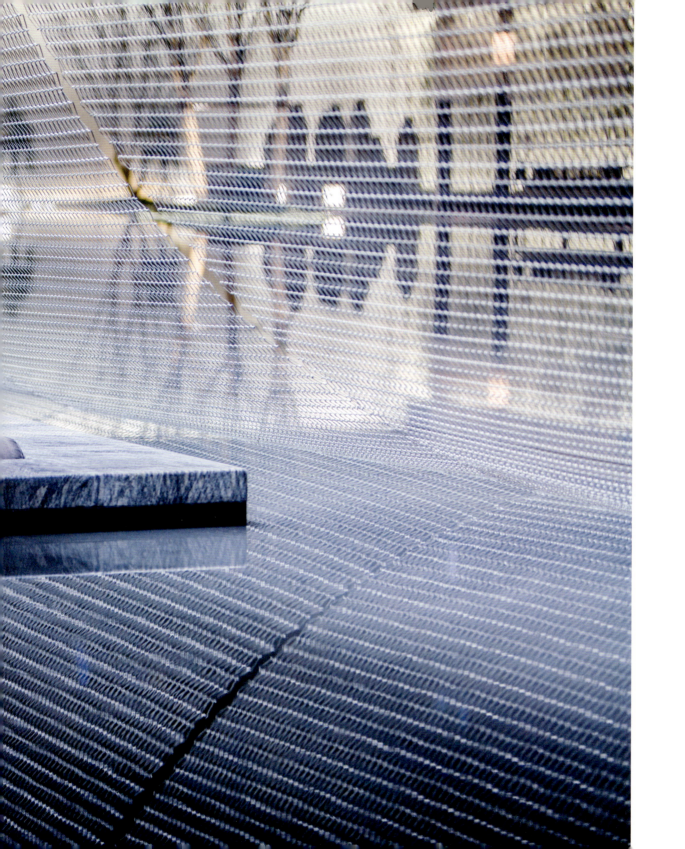

ShuiFa Info Town Property Exhibition Center

**Project Name** ShuiFa Info Town Property Exhibition Center
**Architect or Architecture Firm** aoe
**Architect in Charge** Qun Wen
**Design Team** Gen Li, Shixin Gao, Jiarui Li, Suqing Yan, Liuqing Liu, Ye Wang, Dan Zhu, Jing Du
**Completion Year** 2020
**Built Area** 5,200 m²
**Project Location** Jinan, Shandong, China

The project is located in the Changqing Economic Development Zone, 20 kilometers away from the city centre of Jinan. The area has not yet been developed on a large scale. The surrounding environment is a messy mix of high-voltage line towers dotting weed strewn farmland. In order to give visitors the best viewing experience, the designer has isolated the area from the surrounding environment and has created a relatively enclosed space. The architectural design is inspired by Wang Wei's verse in "Mountain Dwelling in Autumn," "Rain passes in the pristine mountain, refreshing autumn evening. Moon shines among the pine, clear spring flows on stones." Through a four "stones" arrangement, like a stream of clear spring water flowing from the cracks in the rocks. The main structure is assembled out of white perforated panels, glowing with pure and elegant cultural motifs. The northern boundary is designed like a mountain waterfall, combined with green microtopography, giving the whole building an air of refinement filled with cultural significance.

The building's main functions are hosting residential sales expos, property expos, and offices. The main entrance is located on the west side. In order to eliminate the visual impact of the messy surrounding environment, geometrical hills are designed to surround the square, which slowly rises as people enter the site, gradually blocking out the view. Mountains, water, and marble are fused together in this undeveloped wilderness.

A second layer is set outside the main structure – perforated plating, so that the building is enveloped within the perforated plating, forming a relatively enclosed space. The curtain wall sections are slanted, nestled and interlaced inside, and the gap between the sections naturally forms the entrance of the building. Everything happens inside the space covered by the perforated plate curtain wall, connected to the outside world only through the irregular gaps. The interior of the building is obscured by the white perforated plating, and as night falls, light shines through the perforated plates to make the whole building glow, like a piece of shiny marble standing in the wilderness. The density of the perforation of the plate gradually changes from top to bottom according to the function of the building interior. The main function of the first and second floors of the building is as display areas, so the density of perforation is higher for more transparency. The main function of the third and fourth floors of the building is for office space, which requires a relatively private environment, so the number of perforations is lower, and it is relatively more enclosed while ensuring sufficient lighting. The gradual changes in the perforated plates allow the permeability of the building façade to gradually change from top to bottom, giving a sense of depth to the overall surface of the building. The perforated plate itself has a shading effect, like a layer of ecological skin, making the building more environmentally friendly. At the same time, the gray space formed between the glass curtain wall and the perforated plate enriches people's spatial experience inside the building.

In terms of landscape design, in order to reflect the reputation of Jinan as the City of Springs, a large area of cascading water was set up along the main avenue display area, with the water falling from 4-meter-high stone steps. The main entrance to the property exhibition hall is set on the second floor, concealed behind the cascading water, and can be reached through a bridge. On the connecting bridge, there is cascading water on the outside, and a tranquil pool on the inside centered around a welcoming pine. One side is in motion and the other side is tranquil, reflecting the mood of the bright moon shining between the pine tree and clear spring water on the stones. Upon entering the building, visitors are drawn from the wilderness into a paradise.

The interior of the building is also a continuation of the exterior, with the perforated plating element of the entrance area extending directly from the exterior to the interior. A large, four-story atrium serves as a sandbox area and becomes the focal point of the entire space. Natural light comes in from the skylight and is surrounded by perforated plates, forming a space imbued with a sense of ritual. Viewing windows are set up on the enclosed perforated plates, allowing the people upstairs to look over the sandbox, while also setting up a contrast that makes the space livelier.

The integrated design of architecture, view, and interior enables the entire project to be consistent with the design concept. While isolated from the surrounding environment, it also becomes the focal point of the entire area, satisfying the display requirements as an exhibition centre and sales office, bringing new opportunities for the development of this region.

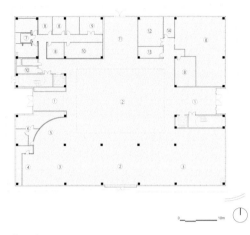

first floor plan

01 lobby
02 model area
03 discussion area
04 bar
05 reception
06 locker room
07 restroom
08 office
09 meeting room
10 equipment room
11 rest area
12 multifunctional room
13 rest room
14 vip room

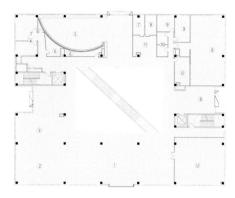

second floor plan

01 model area
02 discussion area
03 display area
04 restroom
05 led display area
06 equipment room
07 smoking room
08 office
09 signing room
10 locker room
11 rest area
12 meeting room

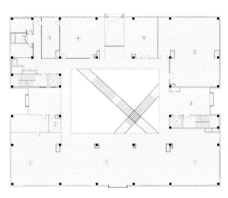

third floor plan

01 display area
02 restroom
03 rest area
04 meeting room
05 multifunctional hall

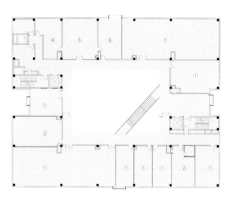

fourth floor plan

01 office
02 meeting room
03 restroom
04 kitchen
05 restaurant
06 dining room

selected works ———— 057

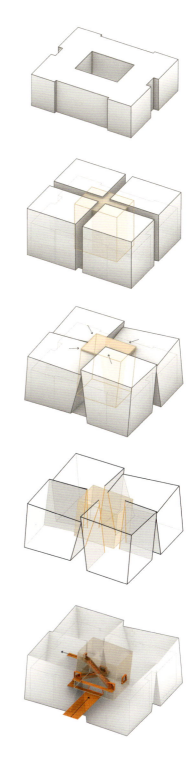

diagram

selected works — 059

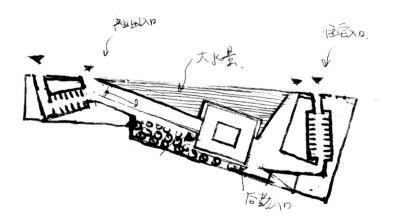

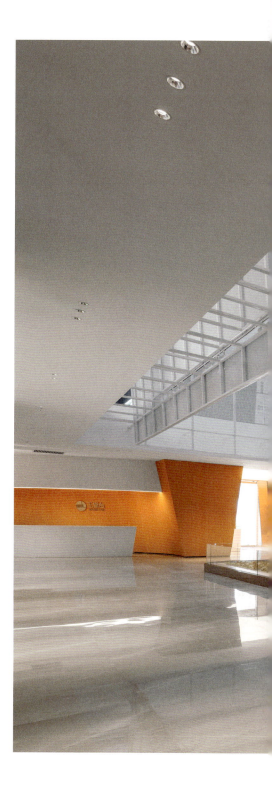

060 ——— aoe Exploring possibilities: A journey of architectural fantasy

selected works ——— 061

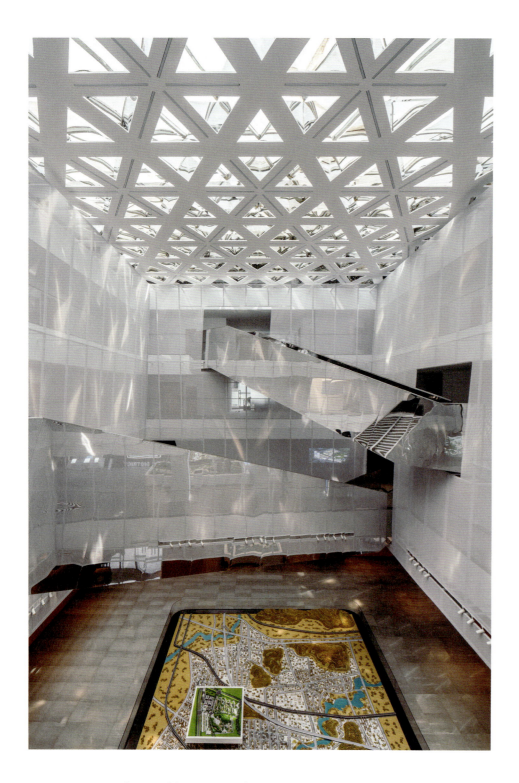

selected works ——— 063

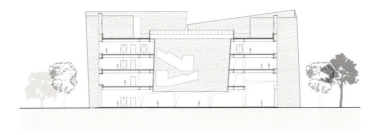

section

068 —— aoe Exploring possibilities: A journey of architectural fantasy

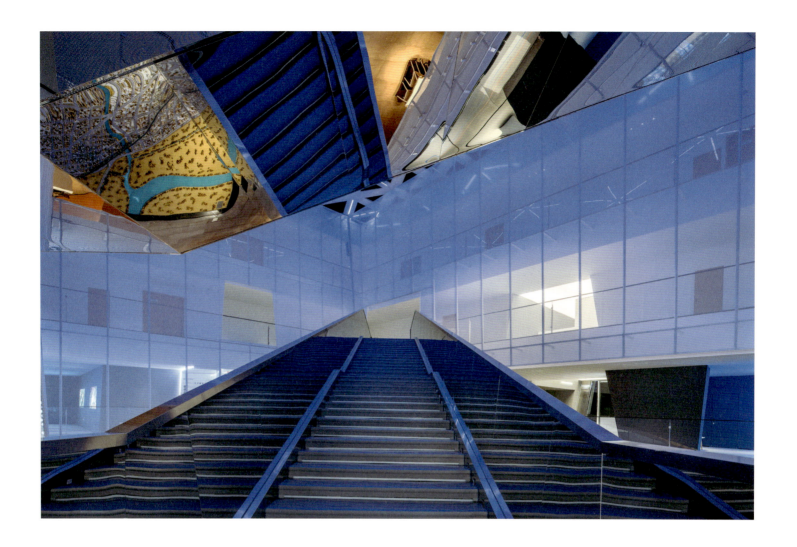

selected works —— 069

selected works —— 073

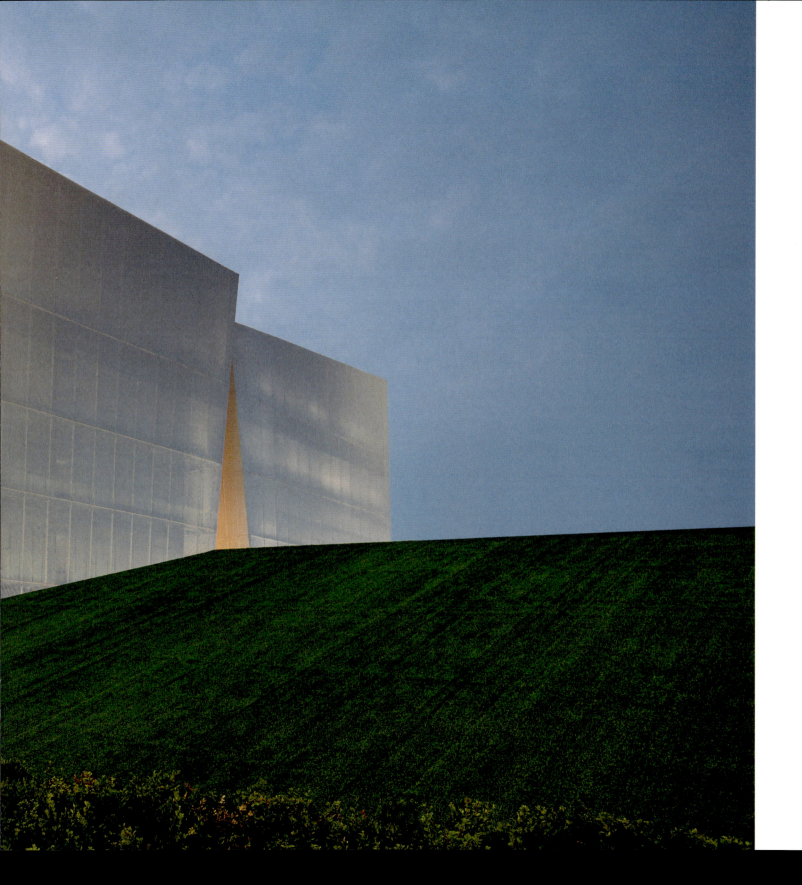

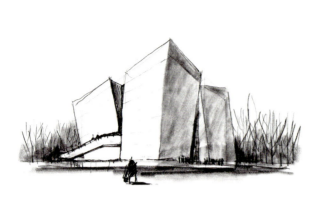

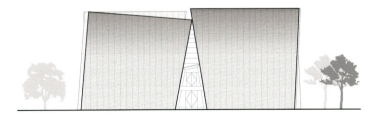

**north elevation**

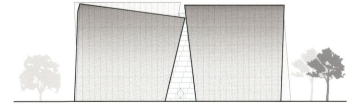

**south elevation**

selected works ———— 079

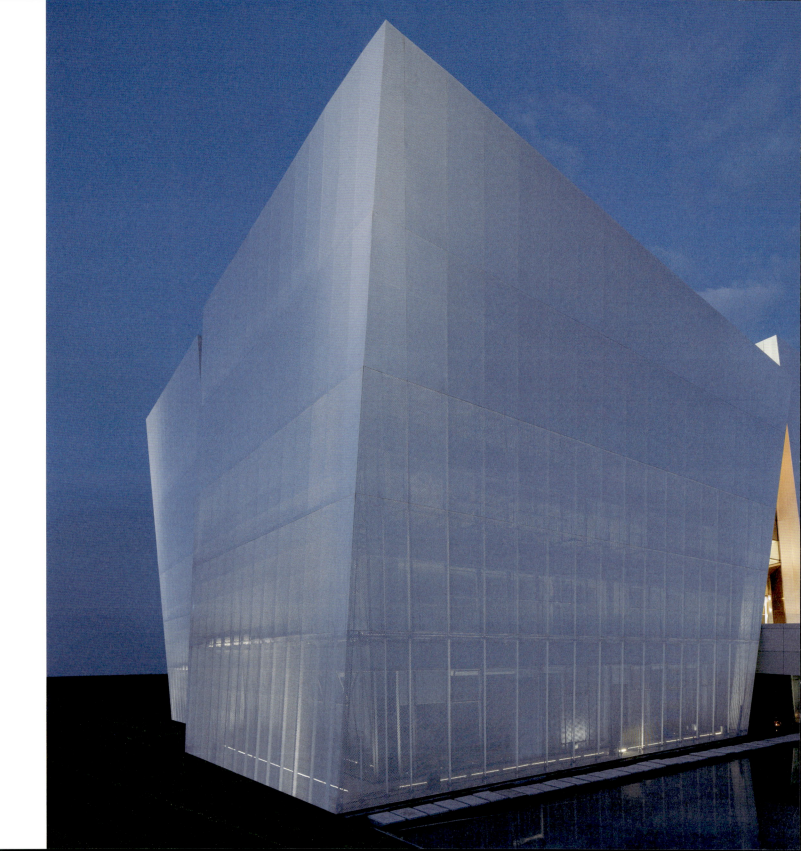

One Sino Park

**Project Name** One Sino Park
**Architecture Firm** aoe
**Architect in Charge** Qun Wen
**Design Team** Shixin Gao, Gen Li, Jiarui Li, Liuqing Liu, Ye Wang
**Completion Year** 2020
**Gross Built Area** 3,210.56 m²
**Project location** Chongqing, China

Located in the northern zone of the core region of Chongqing, China, the project consists of a cliffside building, designed and constructed into its surrounding mountain façade. The main structure has been completed, and designers have deconstructed and reconstructed its internal spaces with an infusion of architectural elements conducive to the topography, resulting in the creation of a rich architectural, urban space. The 3,000m² project consists of four floors. The main entrance is located on the third level, providing access to the main sales center functional areas, including exhibition space, which span the second and third floors. Embracing the sales center, the ground floor features a heated swimming pool and health club, while a small art gallery occupies the fourth floor.

The project highlights relationships between architecture, nature, society, and the people of Chongqing, thus enhancing the spatial experience of the building's visitors through a design-oriented rethinking of modern lifestyles. The concept targets large-scale urban architecture as a conduit for fostering community vitality through public participation and interaction, inspiring people to enhance their life experiences of the future. The open concept of the sales offices breaks with tradition, promoting a more inclusive environment conducive to interaction. The artistic space on the top level will continue to evolve as an integral part of the interactive theme, with plans to develop the space into a community art center in the near future.

Externally, the project incorporates the shapes and forms of surrounding natural rock formations, adapted through deconstructive techniques to create flowing spaces. To complement those elements, the designers carefully studied the characteristics of a wide variety of materials and their effect on shadow and light. Stainless-steel, abundant glass, and acrylic light rods brilliantly contrast with cave-like elements reminiscent of a Roman grotto. The main entrance is supported by a riveted steel structure to form the principal framework. Large sections of wall are cantilevered by steel columns, with composite plates inserted to reduce the overall load. This combination contributes to the irregular freehand brushwork facade of the building's walls. Externally, 800 mm glass cantilevers seamlessly connect the glass framework.

The sculptural building's deconstructivism is highly visible, infusing vibrancy into the city with its splendid artwork and aluminum-formed, thousand-paper crane façade, the latter being a reference to Asian cultural symbolism representing health, longevity, and truth. Stainless-steel plates form the internal workings of the crane system, combined with hanging folded aluminum plates to achieve a dazzling external design. By day, the mirrored finish of the structure's stainless-steel framework glistens in the sunlight, distinguishing itself amongst the surrounding greenery. By night, acrylic light rods emanate brightly, enveloping the structure in a fantastical, dream-like aura. Sculptural design elements further contribute to the building's external visual appeal, positioning it as a work of art that is embraced by the people as a source of civic pride and interaction.

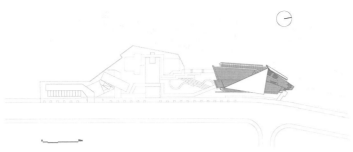

masterplan

masterplan

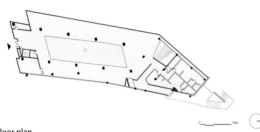

ground floor plan

01  swimming pool   03  men's locker room   05  leisure area
02  women's locker room   04  sauna

second floor plan

01  foyer   03  tearoom   05  reference room
02  office   04  equipment   06  terrace

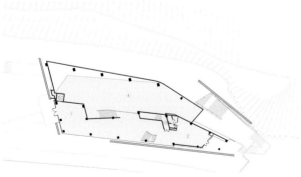

third floor plan

01  lobby   03  equipment
02  hall   04  over the foyer

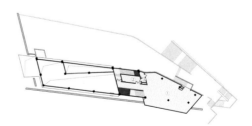

fourth floor plan

01  office   03  equipment
02  reference room   04  over the lobby

selected works ——— 089

sections

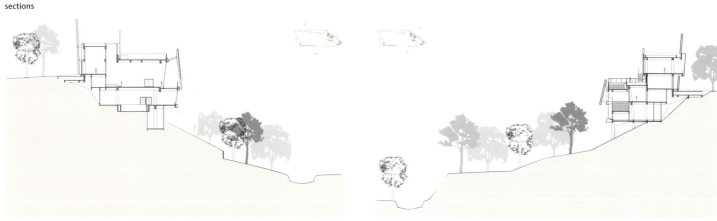

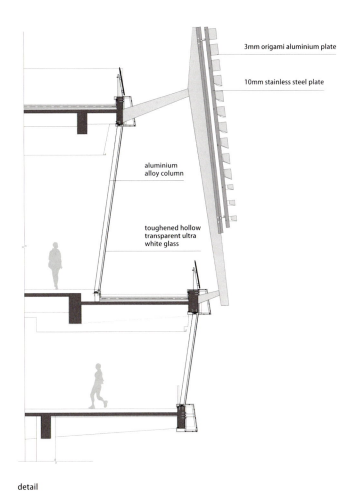

3mm origami aluminium plate

10mm stainless steel plate

aluminium alloy column

toughened hollow transparent ultra white glass

detail

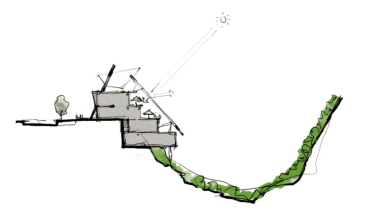

selected works —— 093

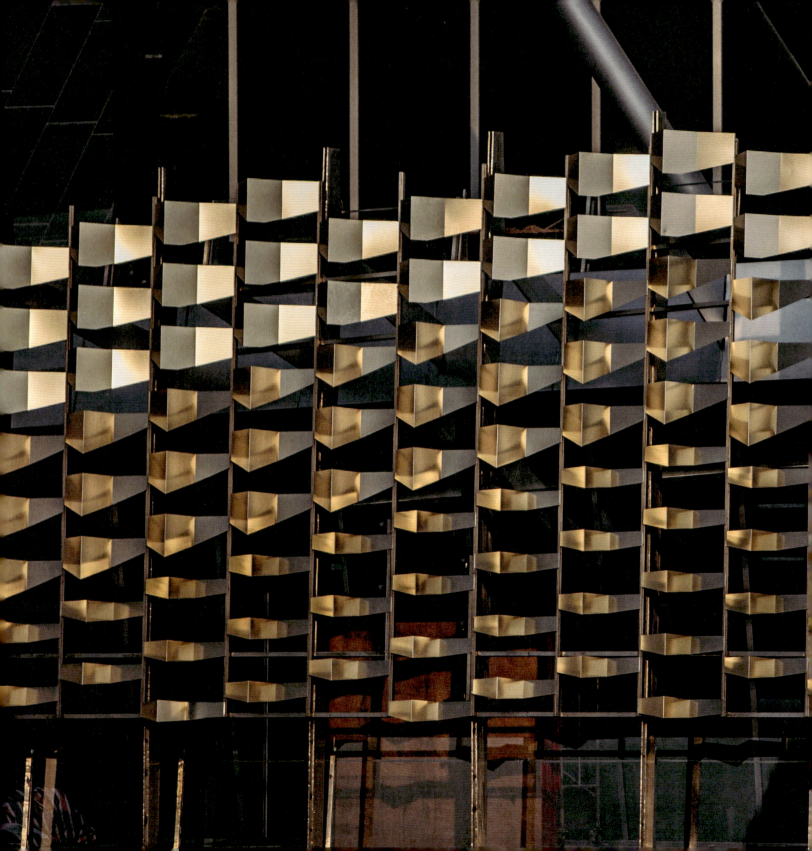

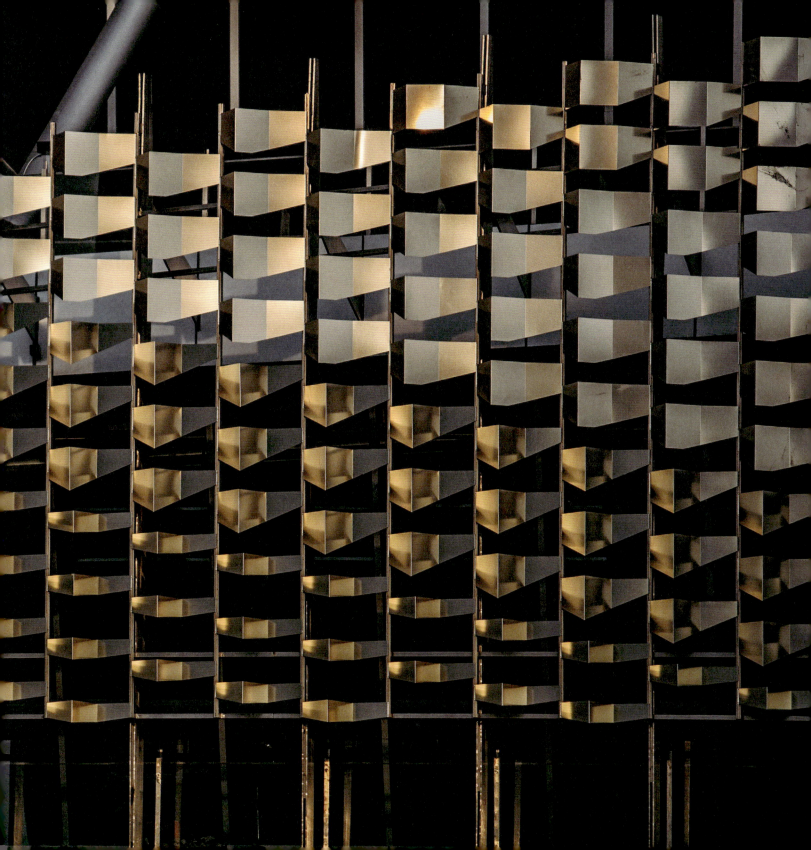

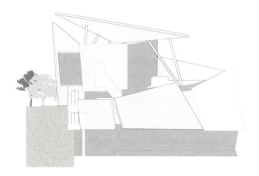

north elevation

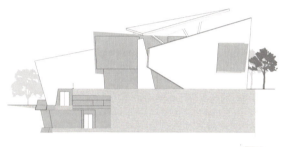

south elevation

selected works ——— 097

selected works —— 099

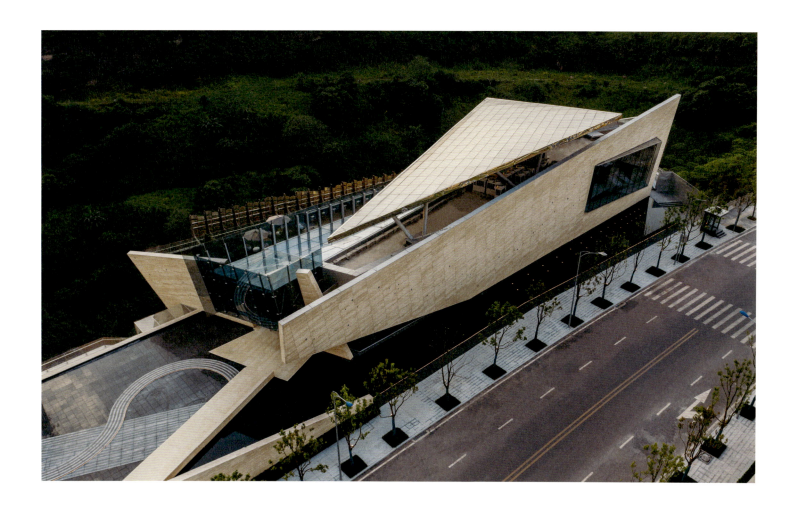

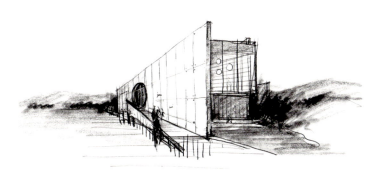

selected works —— 101

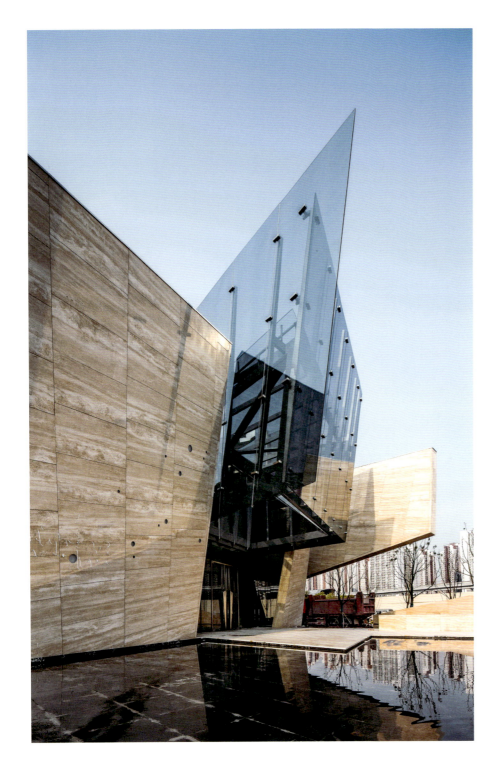

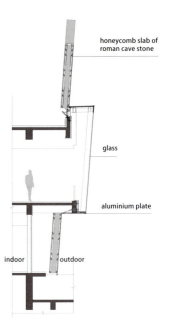

detail section

detail section

selected works — 103

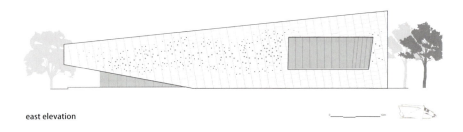

east elevation

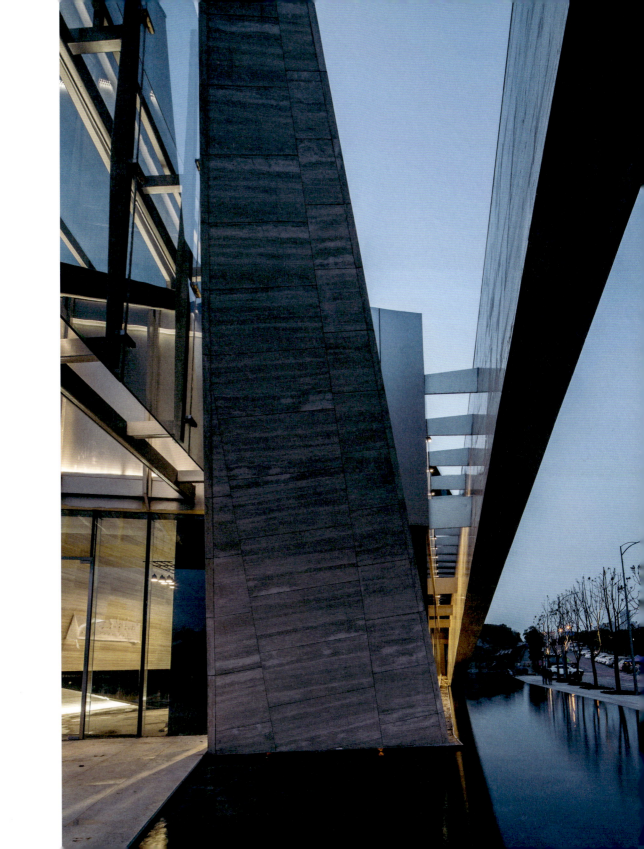

Shanxiao Sales Pavilion

**Project Name** Shanxiao Sales Pavilion
**Architecture Firm** aoe
**Architect in Charge** Qun Wen
**Design Team** Chen Liu, Pengyong Li, Zhuojun Niu, Kaiqi Yang
**Completion Year** 2019
**Gross Built Area** 1,026 m²
**Project location** Chongqing, China

masterplan

Chongqing is a poetic land with half of the city, half of the mountain and trees covering thousands of miles. The project is located in Nanshan, Chongqing. Nanshan located on the south bank of the Yangtze River in Chongqing which has a wealth of tourism resources including natural scenery, cultural landscape, and specialties. In recent years, some commercial buildings have successively appeared with cultural connotations such as bookstores and homestays. These buildings are simple in design and distinctive in shape, which has made Nanshan gradually become a synonym for elegant and introverted. And its artistic conception corresponds to Tao's poetry.

In people's haunt I built my cot;
Of wheel's and hoof's noise, I hear not.
How can it leave on me no trace?
Secluded heart makes a secluded place.
I pick fence-side asters at will;
Carefree I see the southern hill.
The mountain air's fresh day and night;
Together birds go home in flight.
What revelation at this view?
Words fail me if I try to tell you.
——Yuanming Tao

Therefore, we refine the traditional architectural culture and natural landscape of Nanshan as the main tempo, and use modern technical language and artistic creation techniques to transform it into our architectural language, so that visitors can experience the artistic conception of "hidden in the nature."

The entire project has two parts, the sales office and the commercial part. The sales office has a small scale but exquisite and delicate. It is naturally engraved and hidden in nature, thus highlighting the concept of "seclusion." The façade uses the perforated plate as the louver to protect from the sunshine, and the shape of the louver is inspired by the cloud of Nanshan. The perforated leaves float around the curtain wall. It resembles a long scroll landscape painting, and its changes show the shape of the clouds and fog that stretches in Nanshan. The glass curtain walls with gradual mist and perforated louvers are integrated so that the whole building seems to be floating in the clouds. At the same time, there are spraying devices that will create fog around the building every day. It makes the natural fog become another layer of façade for the building, creating a wonderland of Nanshan. The building is not only an architectural but a cultural event.

For the commercial architecture, we researched the characteristics and scale of the mountain building and abandoned the majesty created by the large volume and the large scale. We combined the living space of the residents through the appropriate scale and open and relaxed corridor space, neighboring habits, modern literary and artistic life needs to create more dialogues between people and people, between people and nature. The pleasant scale makes people feel as if they are in nature and walk in the alleys, thus staying in it becomes a kind of returning to the original, leisurely and unique enjoyment. The choice of building façade color comes from traditional dwellings and blends in with the natural environment. The choice of the color of the building façade comes from the traditional dwellings. The light and shadow effect formed by the light on the pure "white box" gives the viewer a pure visual enjoyment. It stands in harmony with the natural environment and disappears into everything.

 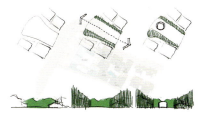 

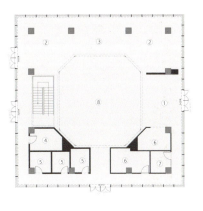

ground floor plan

01 entrance
02 wc
03 office
04 meeting room
05 discussion area
06 equipment room
07 brand display area
08 water bar
09 book bar

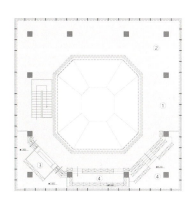

second floor plan

01 display area
02 discussion area
03 water bar
04 library

selected works ——— 113

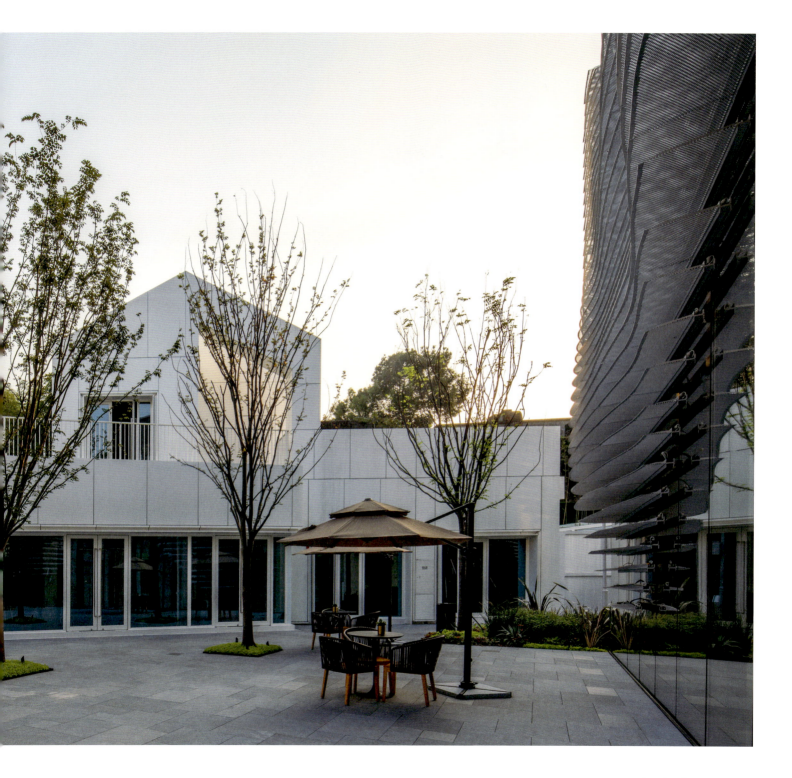

selected works ——— 115

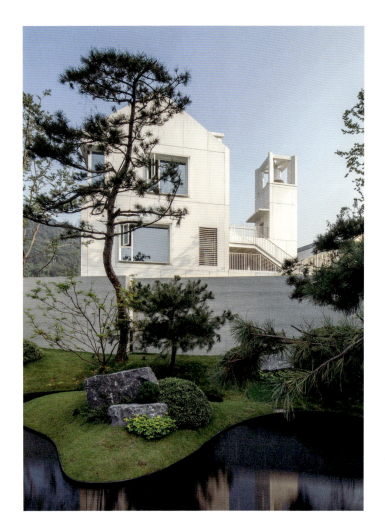

selected works —— 117

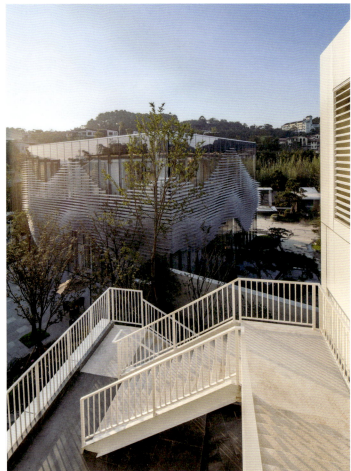

selected works ——— 119

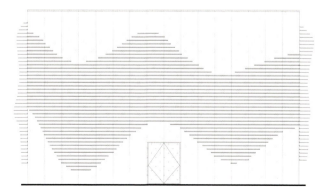

elevation

selected works — 121

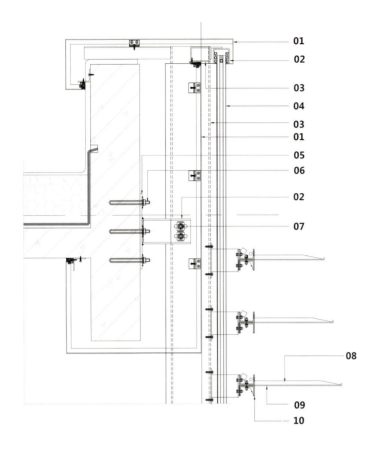
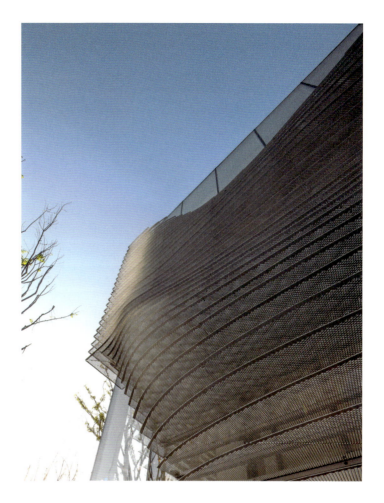
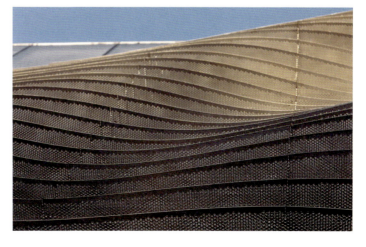

detailed drawing of punched aluminium plate wall body

01 thick aluminium veneer
02 hot-dip galvanized channel steel
03 steel moment tube
04 tempered ultra white hollow glass
05 galvanized steel sheet
06 chemical anchor bolt
07 stainless steel bolt
08 side edgefold
09 thick perforated aluminium plate
10 channel aluminium stiffener

selected works —— 125

selected works — 129

130 ——— aoe Exploring possibilities: A journey of architectural fantasy

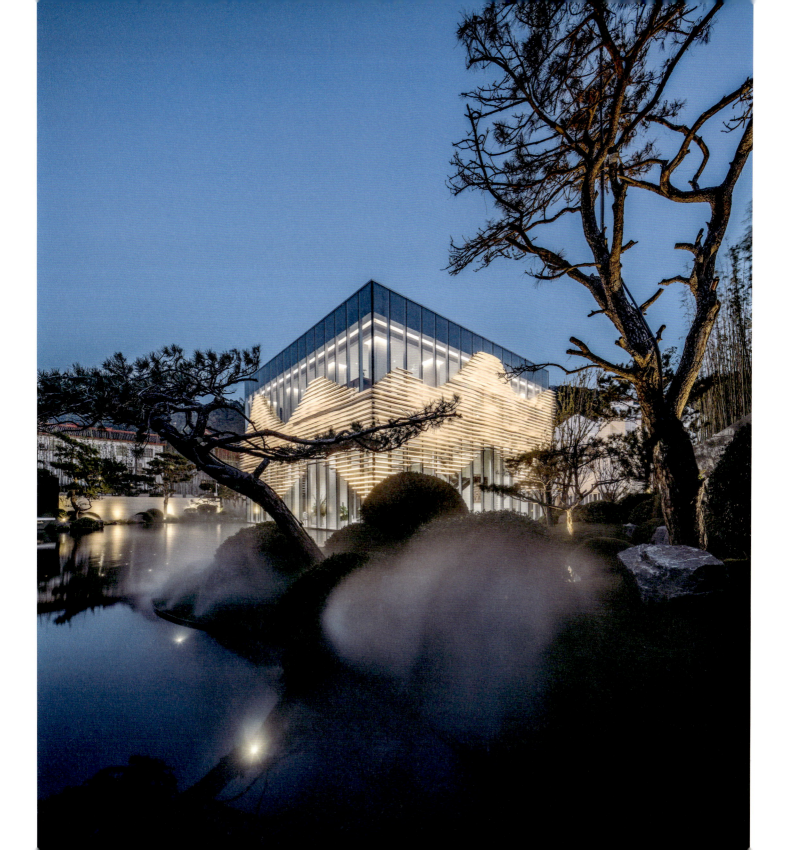

Sino-Italian Culture Exchange City Reception Center

**Project Name** Sino-Italian Culture Exchange City Reception Center
**Architecture Firm** aoe
**Architect in Charge** Qun Wen
**Design Team** Jianning Ma, Ruixue Fan, Ye Wang, Zhiyu Chang, Jichang Pan, Xiangting Li, Yu Lu
**Completion Year** 2021
**Gross Built Area** 1,695.8 m²
**Project location** Chengdu, Sichuan, China

Chengdu, hailed as the land of abundance, has a civilization history of 4,500 years and a city construction history of 2,300 years. In the 13th century, Marco Polo came to Chengdu, and the Corridor Bridge, the Jinjiang River and the cloth of ancient Sichuan became the most colorful parts of his travelogue. In the 21st century, against the background of the Belt and Road Initiative, the planning of Chengdu Tianfu Cultural and Creative City came into being, and the Sino-Italian Cultural and Artistic Exchange Center is an important part of the City, aiming to build a platform for cultural exchange and civilization interchange between the two countries. The project is planned to cover an area of 17813 square meters, with a construction area of 2,106.7 square meters. The site is located about 36 kilometers from the center of Chengdu, on the north side of Wenchuang Road 10, next to Tianfu Avenue, with a good display. At the platform of the exhibition hall, you can take a look at the creative group projects on the east side and the natural landscape of Yanqi Wetland.

At the beginning of the design, the architects hoped to find the intersection of the two in the cultural differences between the East and the West: the overall design concept was taken from the "Ruyi," which has been used in China since ancient times as a gift to foreign ambassadors to signify the conclusion of friendly relations and the peace of the two countries; while the Italian pavilion draws its design inspiration from Italy's most representative piazza, shaping an intimate and pleasantly scaled urban art living room. The design elements are extracted from ancient Roman arches and domes, and the smooth enclosure of multiple circular squares is used to form a rich and versatile use space to meet the multifunctional requirements of exhibition, meeting, reception and catering. The use of pure white on all walls gives the building a different three-dimensional light effect in the sunlight, while the large area of glass extends the indoor space

to the outside and allows the outdoor scenery to be fully mapped in, becoming a dynamic mural of the four seasons. With the change of wall materials, the designer creates the feeling of space that is both inside and outside, and the pavilion is thus perfectly integrated into the surrounding natural environment. The inside is still inside, the outside is still outside, but the spiritual feelings and aspirations are boundless inside and outside.

The harmony between architecture and nature lies in the use of natural resources as well as in the protection of the natural environment. The pavilions on both sides are designed with top lighting, so that the light is evenly diffused in the indoor and outdoor spaces. In addition, the introduction of multilevel outdoor greenery and the use of buoyant ventilation devices to channel airflow into the building organically combine the natural elements of light, scenery and wind, allowing people to perceive and coexist with the surrounding natural environment while they are in the building. Meanwhile, the building design reveres the existing ecological environment and uses materials and means such as low-e glass, local wood and green roofs to reduce building energy consumption and achieve sustainable construction. The exhibition hall serves as an important part for linking and integrating the surrounding ecological forest.

In terms of space planning, the designer has reserved the most flexible space for exhibition and display. The staggered height of the building allows visitors to stand at different heights and view different scenery, creating a "walk in the woods" mood and a unique experience.

The interior of the building is a flowing space shaped by 10 circular walls of different sizes, which are divided into three levels of elevation

ground floor plan

01 entrance lobby
02 cloak room
03 lobby
04 meeting room
05 exhibition room
06 multifunction room
07 outdoor theater
08 italian plaza
09 outdoor corridor
10 service room
11 toilet

roof plan

01 roof plan
02 east garden
03 chirico space
04 service platform

in accordance with the terrain, rising from the entrance hall to the interior space step by step, with two circular skylights in the entrance hall and the central exhibition hall to guide visitors from the entrance hall to the main exhibition hall. The ceiling is controlled at the same level, and the height of the space is richly varied. Except for the round solid wall, the interior and exterior boundaries are all glass, fully incorporating the outdoor landscape into the interior and the natural landscape as part of the exhibition in the form of framed scenery.

The circular space consists of two spatial forms: indoor and piazza; three outdoor semi-circular piazzas are defined as the entrance fountain piazza, the Italian piazza, and the outdoor theater, each reproducing a typical Italian urban piazza space. The Piazza Italia is surrounded by the ruins of the Roman arches. The three indoor circular spaces are designed as a meeting hall, a multifunctional hall and a multimedia showroom, which are arranged around the central exhibition hall. By controlling the size of the circular wall openings, the light and darkness of the space is defined, while the meeting room is surrounded by water features and sculptures. The other five outdoor semi-circular walls are surrounded by greenery and mountains, facing nature.

The visitor crosses the gable to the Italian piazza and ascends a curved staircase to the roof garden. There are two circular gardens, one in the east and one in the west, which are complemented by the contrast between natural vegetation and stone.

The Chinese Cultural Hall on the east side is reached by walking down through the cultural corridor or stepping over the Chinese white jade pavement above the water pond. The two paths symbolize the two Silk Roads between East and West, on land and on water.

selected works —— 139

selected works —— 141

142 ——— aoe Exploring possibilities: A journey of architectural fantasy

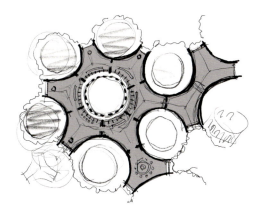

selected works ———— 143

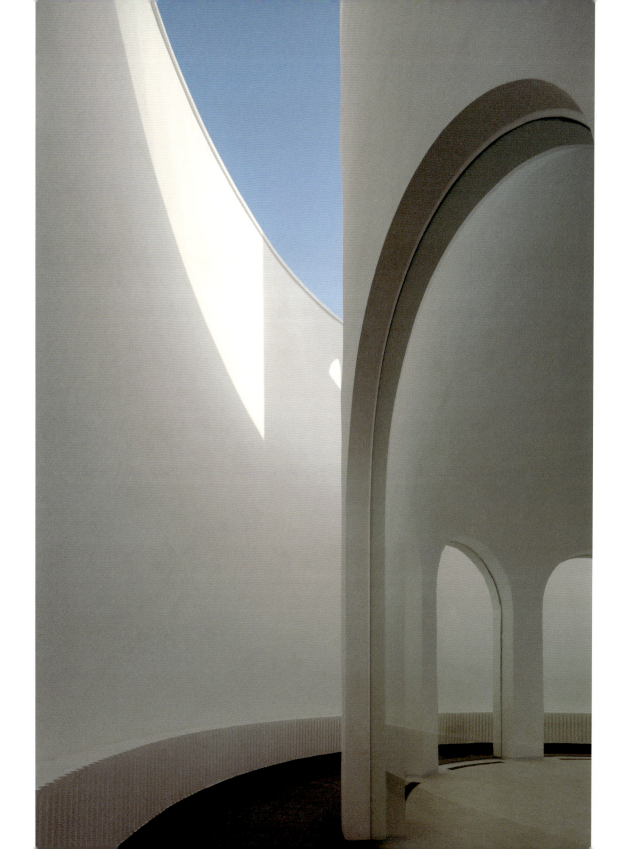

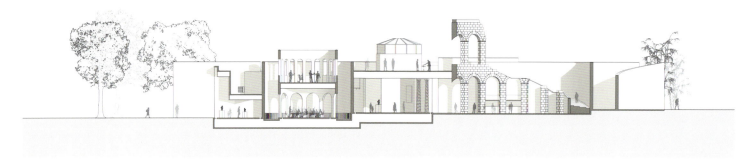

section

148 ——— aoe Exploring possibilities: A journey of architectural fantasy

selected works ——— 149

selected works —— 155

aoe  Exploring possibilities: A journey of architectural fantasy

selected works ——— 161

Sino-Italian Culture Exchange City
Reception Center - The Chinese Cultural Hall

**Project Name** Sino-Italian Culture Exchange City Reception Center -
The Chinese Cultural Hall
**Architecture Firm** aoe
**Architect in Charge** Qun Wen
**Design Team** Jianning Ma, Ruixue Fan, Ye Wang, Zhiyu Chang,
Jichang Pan, Xiangting Li
**Completion Year** 2021
**Built Area** 353.9 m²
**Project location** Chengdu, Sichuan, China

The Chinese Cultural Hall is located to the east of the Sino-Italian Cultural Exchange Center. It can be reached from the Sino-Italian Pavilion through the cultural corridor surrounded by bamboo forests. The Chinese Cultural Hall is composed of multifunctional halls, meeting rooms, restaurants, piano pavilions and tea rooms, the design is full of oriental charm.

At the beginning of the design, the architect hoped to find the intersection of the two in the form of Chinese and Western cultural differences: the overall layout concept of the site was taken from the "Ruyi" that China used to gift foreign envoys since ancient times to signify the establishment of friendly relations and imply the peace of the two countries. The east and west pavilions are connected by a cultural corridor, it surrounded by ponds and bamboo forests. The Chinese Cultural Hall and the Chinese-Italian Cultural Hall use Italian squares as their spatial prototypes. Through the creation of scenery, form, meaning and emotion, they interpret the cultural philosophy of the harmony between man and nature in the Eastern world.

Scenery: The original site of the site is a bamboo forest with a pond on the west side. The starting point is to preserve the bamboo forest as much as possible and integrate the building into the bamboo forest. The functions are scattered throughout the bamboo forest, and the courtyard wall separates the inner and outer courtyards. Three courtyards are interspersed inside, so that the indoor space, courtyard and bamboo forest form a tendency to look at each other. A Chinese-style modern landscape garden is arranged in the courtyard to create a unique interior landscape. Stepping into the bamboo forest, stepping down, the piano room hidden under the bamboo forest is looming, the sound of the piano, the sound of wind, the

swaying sound of bamboo leaves and the light and shadow dancing under the bamboo forest are integrated. Out of the bamboo forest, the tea room floats above the pond, full of sunlight, suddenly enlightened, and looking to the west, the Zhongyi Pavilion is reflected in the quiet water lily pond.

Form: The architectural form adopts a traditional wooden frame to carry out modern translation and uses circular geometric elements. The continuous cross-shaped arch column extends from the interior to the exterior and the transparent glass curtain wall eliminates the boundary between the interior and the exterior, naturally bringing the outdoor scenery into the interior. The outdoor continuous circular hollow corridor frame creates a varied and quiet light and shadow experience. The courtyard wall extends from the cultural corridor, passing through the bamboo forests, connecting the houses in series, resembling the freehand brushwork and relaxation of Chinese calligraphy. The opposite view window hole on the courtyard wall is shaped like a drop of water, taking the meaning of nature.

Meaning: The Chinese Cultural Hall is composed of houses, courtyards, corridors, and landscapes. "Scenery" is an inseparable element of architecture. Architecture originates from scenery, is derived from scenery, merges with scenery, and eventually becomes a part of scenery. It fully embodies the Eastern wisdom of Taoism, nature, and the unity of man and nature.

Passion: Through respect and use of nature, the Chinese Culture Hall integrates the space with natural elements such as light, wind, sound and smell to form an emotional memory that gives oriental charm. At the same time, it is also the best presentation of Sino-Italian cultural exchanges.

site plan

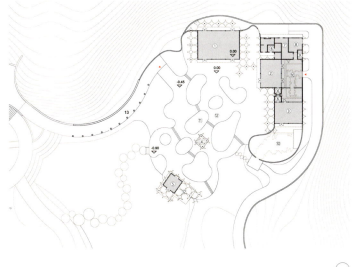

ground floor plan

01  multifunctional room
02  meeting room
03  restaurant
04  qin pavilion
05  tea room

06  toilet
07  kitchen
08  store room
09  mep
10  courtyard

11  bamboo forest
12  deck
13  culture corridor

selected works ——— 169

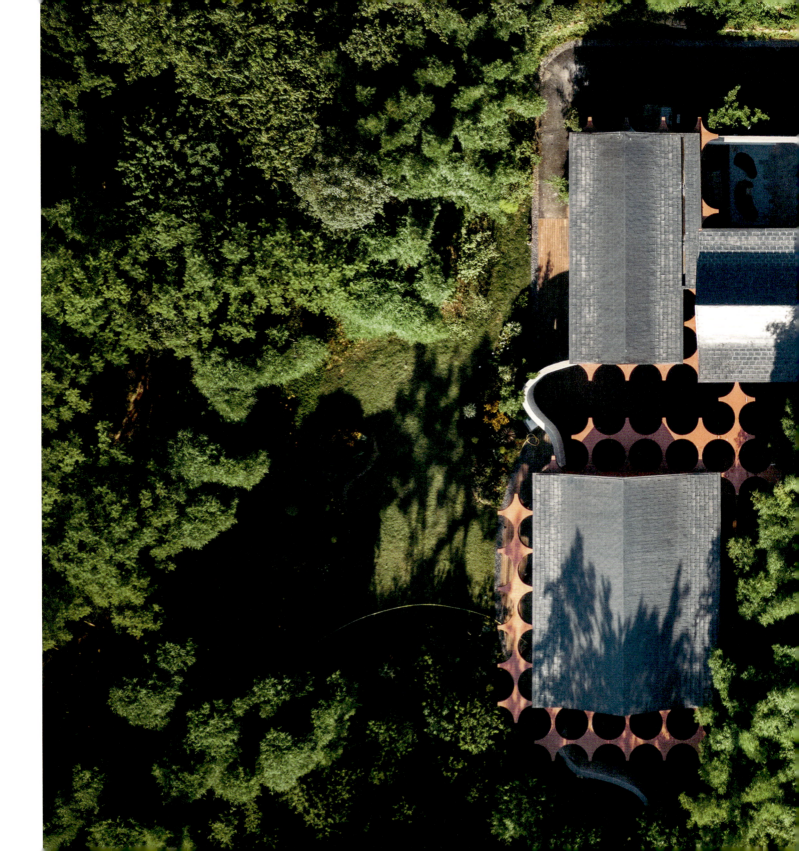

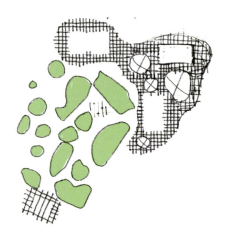

selected works —— 179

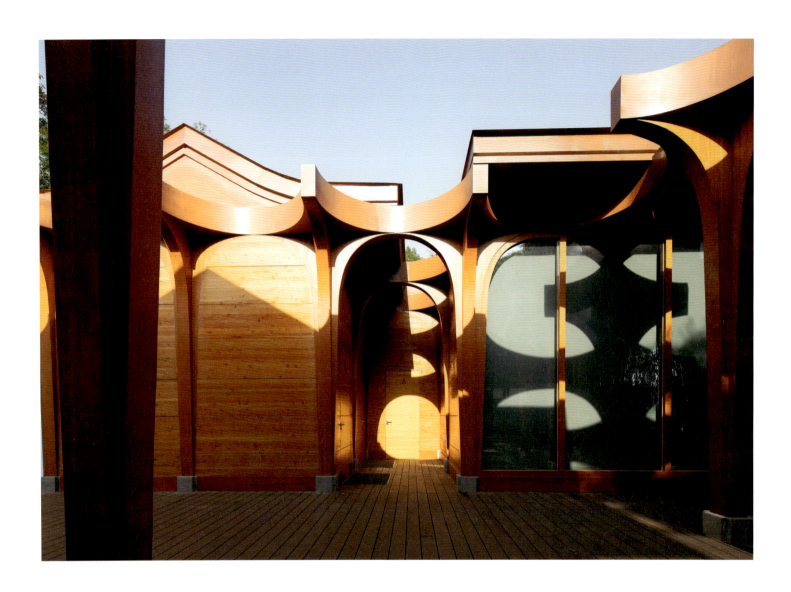

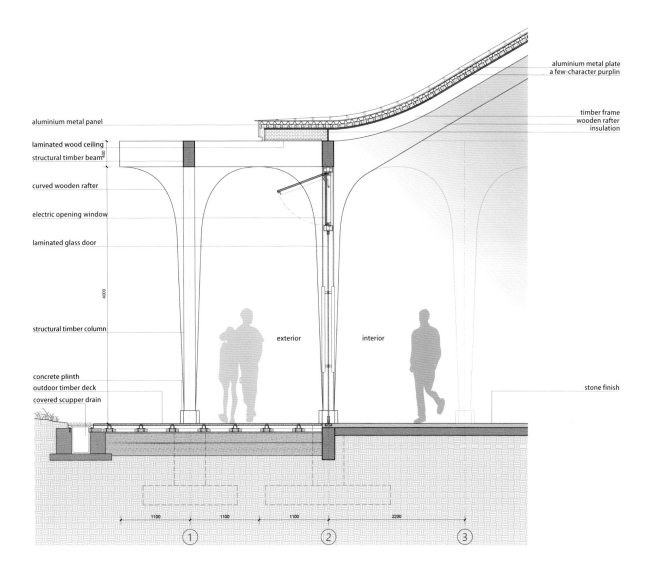

detail section

selected works — 185

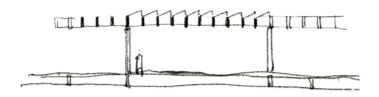

selected works

south elevation

a-a section

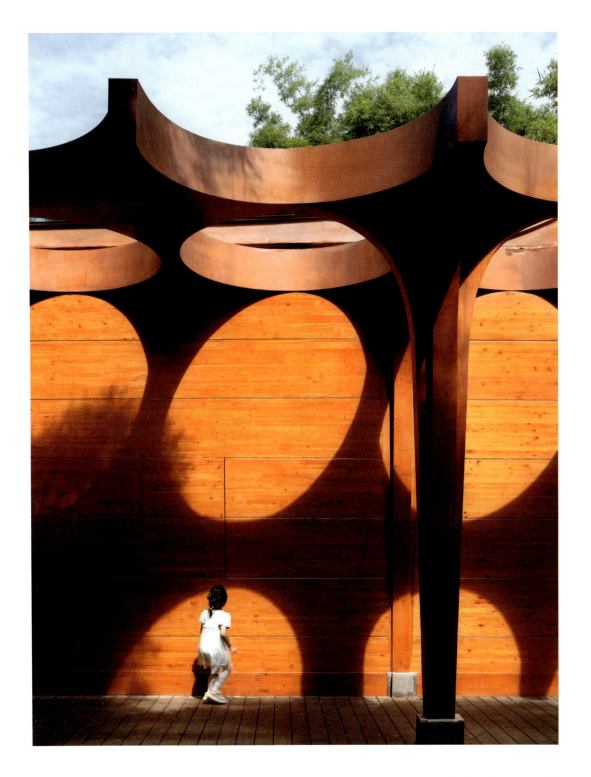

selected works —— 191

Courtyard No. 1 Heze

**Project Name** Courtyard No. 1 Heze
**Architect or Architecture Firm** aoe
**Architect in Charge** Qun Wen
**Design Team** Mingwang Huo,Gen Li, Jing Du, Chen Du, Kaiqi Yang,
Xiaodan Chang, Zhuojun Niu
**Completion Year** 2019
**Built Area** 1,560 m²
**Project Location** Heze, Shandong, China

As China's development and urbanization continues, property developers have begun to expand into new markets such as third and fourth-tier cities. Sales offices have become an important conduit for them to demonstrate their brand's strength and design philosophy. These offices are not only community activity centers and lounge areas for client communication, but also a promotional window to attract more clients to buy properties.

After most of the properties have been sold, however, the usefulness of these offices declines. The purpose of this project is to reconsider the special function of the sales office building, in hopes of making it more sustainable through design, by becoming a symbolic public building for the future community and city.

This project is situated at the intersection of Guangzhou Road and Minjiang Road in the Economic Development Zone of Heze City in Shandong. It will become the new CBD center of Heze. Due to its unique location, the project is expected to be a landmark building in the future development of this prefecture-level city. We hope, through the concept of humanity and sustainability, to express the city's future yearning for a better life, and to provide to local residents an impressive public space.

The architectural concept is based on the artistic supremacism that reflected the social and technological changes of the 1920s, with the intention of expressing the mutual influence and interdependence between physical and virtual space in the digital age.

In the digital age, many of today's actions are performed in the virtual world. Therefore, the objects in the building are designed to float in an unstable state. Each object echoes a corresponding function in a unique form, including the entrance (horseshoe), model area (big camera lens), enterprise brand (blue stone), office area (orange-colored box), etc.

Objects floating in the air form a rich and hierarchical space, welcoming the surrounding audiences with an open dynamic posture. Some of the objects collide with the glass surface and leave traces to form a unique architectural image. The building façade is made of ultra-white glass which makes objects, spaces, material, and color from the interior visible to the outside space.

masterplan

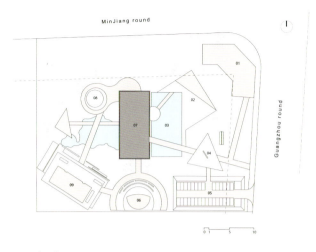

site plan

01 L shaped plaza    06 amphitheatre
02 square plaza      07 sales office
03 pool              08 playground
04 triangular plaza  09 mockup room
05 car park

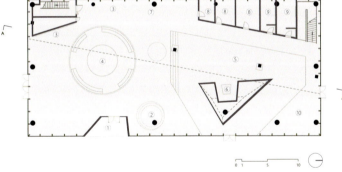

first floor plan

01 entrance          07 exhibition area
02 reception         08 led screen
03 brand display area 09 exhibition area
04 model area        10 office
05 discussion area   11 wc
06 bar               12 vip area

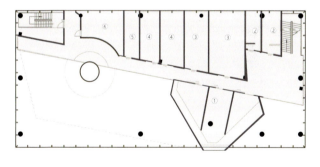

second floor plan

01 signing room
02 wc
03 office
04 meeting room
05 storage
06 equipment room

selected works ——— 207

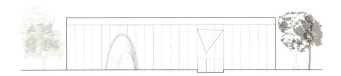

east elevation

north elevation

208 ——— aoe Exploring possibilities: A journey of architectural fantasy

selected works —— 209

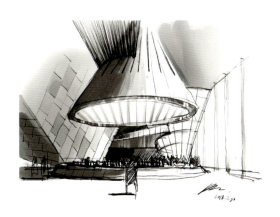

selected works ——— 211

212 ——— aoe Exploring possibilities: A journey of architectural fantasy

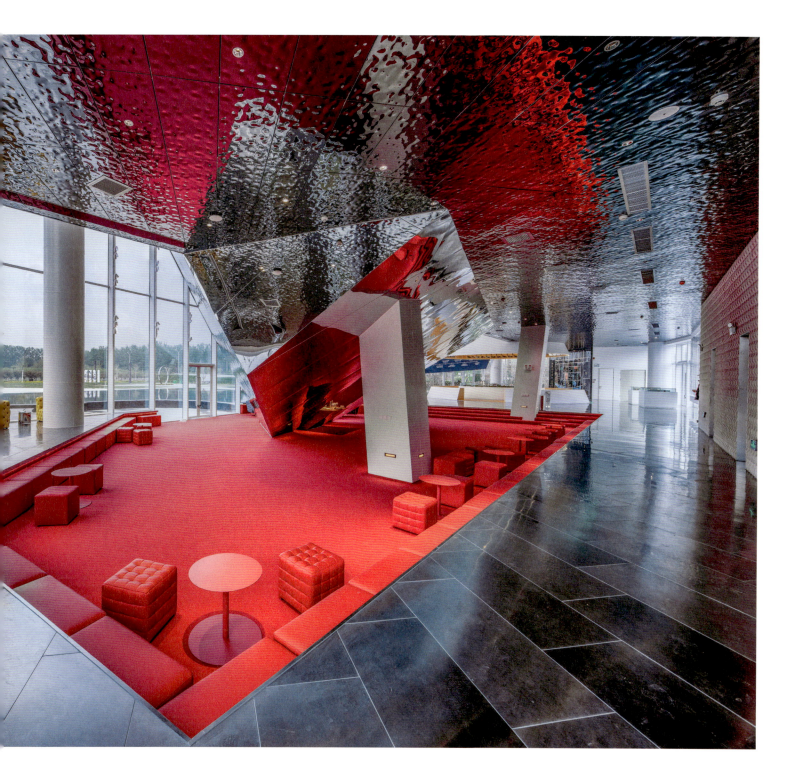

selected works —— 215

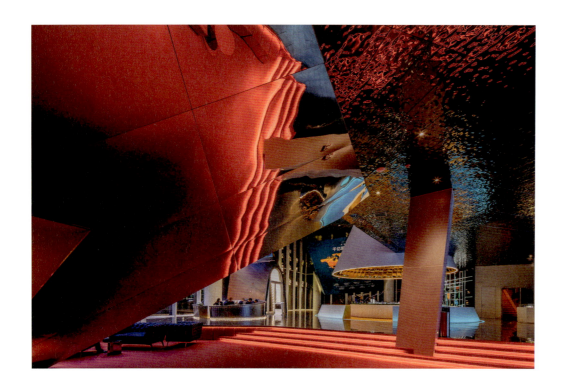

216 ——— aoe  Exploring possibilities: A journey of architectural fantasy

selected works — 217

01 yellow autimotive metallic paint
02 mirror stainless steel plate
03 white fluorocarbon paint
04 led light
05 white acrylic panel

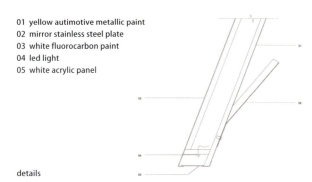

details

01 led
02 partial perforation
03 galvanized steel tube
04 mt-05 dark grey matte metal panel

detail

selected works — 219

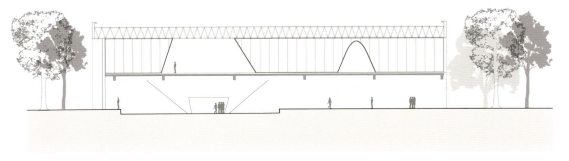

a-a section

selected works —— 221

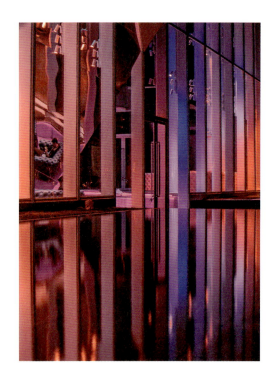
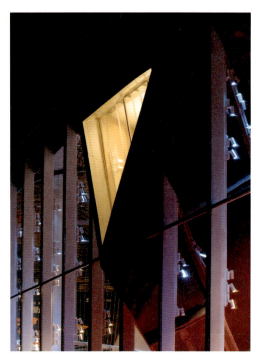
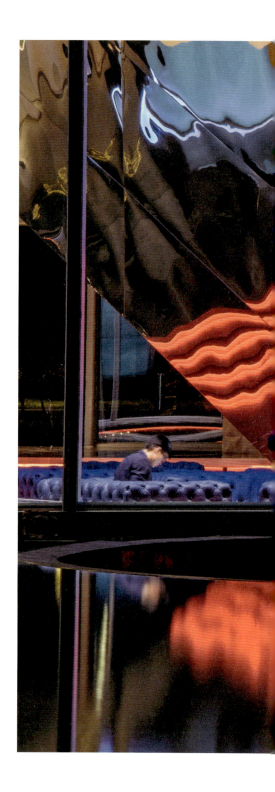

222 ——— **aoe** Exploring possibilities: A journey of architectural fantasy

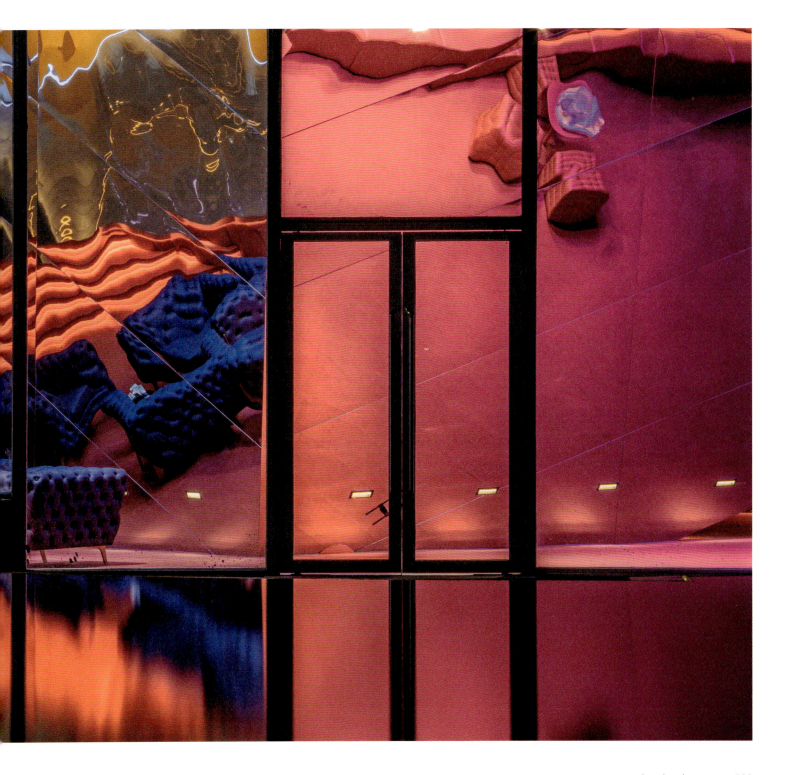

selected works — 223

Haikou International Duty Free Reception Center

**Project Name** Haikou International Duty Free Reception Center
**Architect or Architecture Firm** aoe
**Architect in Charge** Qun Wen
**Design Team** Jianning Ma, Xiao Tang, Qing Liu,Chen Liu
**Completion Year** 2021
**Built Area** 2,215 m²
**Project Location** Haikou, China

Architecture, which appeared in the Stone Age, uses the basic structure of wind to provide people with shelter from rain. On the basis of functionality, the pursuit of more spiritual soul is injected. The building, located in the Haikou Binhai New Area, is not only a characteristic sales center also a modern art gallery. It is the gateway to the west coast city and the spiritual fortress of this area.

In the design, we use deconstructionist techniques to dismantle and reorganize the building wall, release the form and volume and then realize the infinite possibilities of space by interspersing the blocks. The integration of the style school abstracts and simplifies the architecture, to make it an artistic element.

We increased the thickness of the outer wall to emphasize it and form a strong architectural symbol. At the same time, windows and platforms are inserted into the wall to open the covered building to the city, it also introduces urban events into the building and becomes a place for the public to create events.

The addition of circular elements emphasizes the geometrical sense of the building more. The curved wall is displayed at the opening of the outer wall, and completely different materials are used to form a visual focus on the façade. The interior is also interspersed with blocks of different shapes, forming a rich and varied space.

In the choice of façade color, we considered the city of Haikou's climate characteristics of warm and comfortable all year round and sufficient sunshine and chose white as the main color to make the building brighter and more refreshing visually. The large area of the white wall is like a pure canvas and the light and shadow are like pen and ink. Painting on the wall is like the blank in traditional Chinese painting.

For the material of the elevation, horizontal-grained panels and titanium-zinc panels are used as embellishments on the protruding walls and curved walls of the building. The white of the cross-grained board and the gray of the titanium-zinc board collide with each other, forming a strong contrast. The texture of the two materials is derived from the skin of the dried palm which makes the building more textured and echoes the surrounding natural environment.

The project is functionally divided into two major areas, marketing area and investment promotion area. In order to achieve the relative independence of the two functional areas and the integrity of the building, we arranged the volume in an L shape. The marketing area is arranged along the main road and is more open. The negotiation area on the first floor uses a large area of glass, the space is bright and transparent and the interior scene is shown to pedestrians. The good accessibility allows pedestrians to easily participate in the activities inside the building.

Compared with the marketing area, the overall investment zone is relatively closed to ensure the privacy of visitors. The function of the investment promotion part is developed along the city's secondary arterial road. On the side of the street interface, the real wall is used to isolate the noise and the view opens on the side facing the inner courtyard. Visitors enter the interior of the building through a cylinder of titanium-zinc plates. A terrace is set on the second floor to enjoy the view of the inner courtyard and the entire area.

site plan

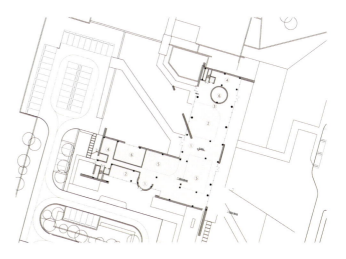

ground floor plan

01 reception  03 bar  05 model area
02 discussion area  04 rest room  06 vip room

second floor plan

01 office  03 meeting room  05 balcony
02 vip room  04 rest room

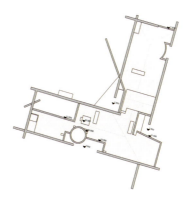

roof plan

selected works —— 231

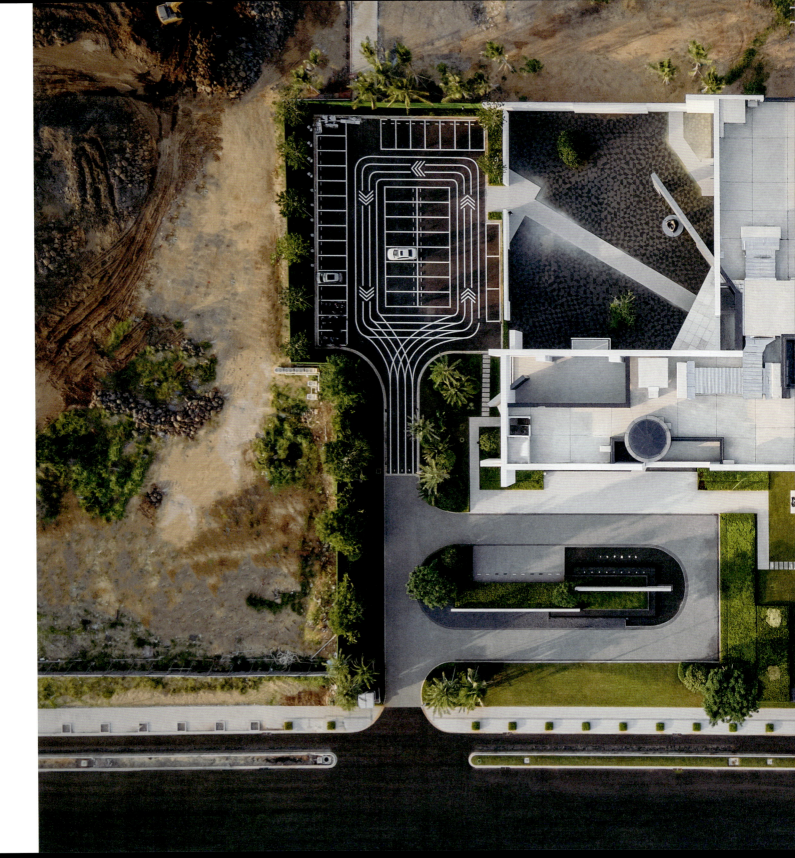

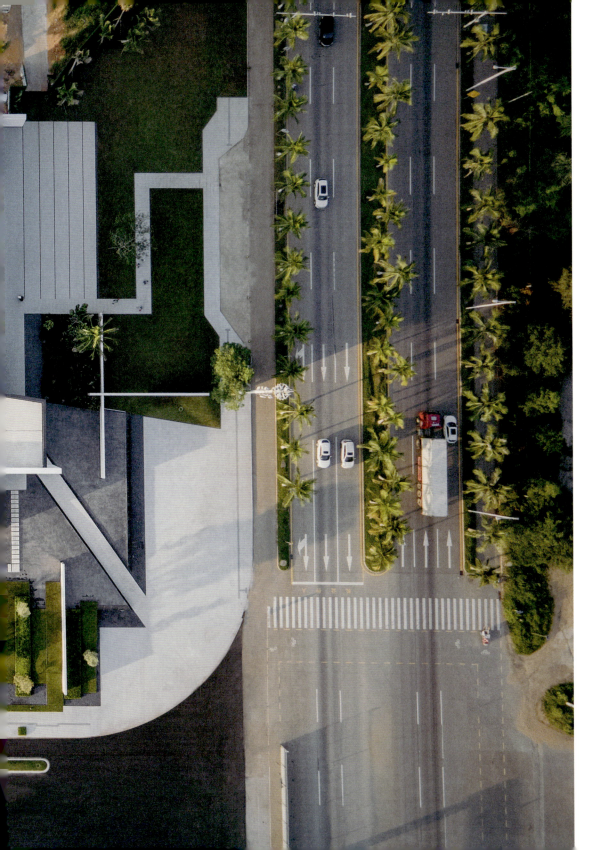

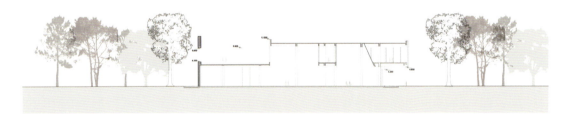

section

east elevation

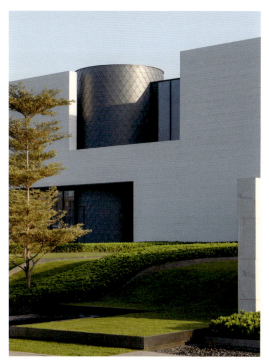

selected works ——— 239

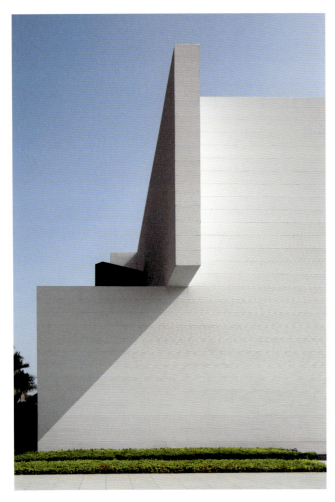

selected works —— 243

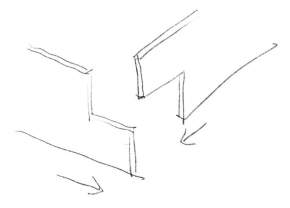

selected works — 247

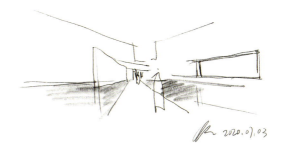

selected works

west elevation

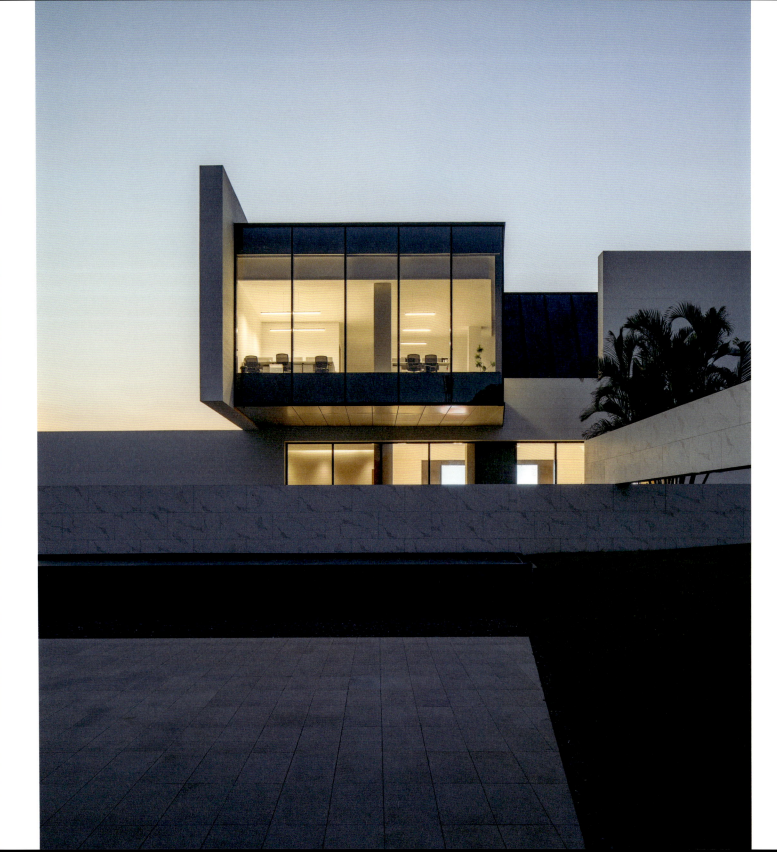

Heze Nanjing Road Sales Office

**Project Name** Heze Nanjing Road Sales Office
**Architect or Architecture Firm** aoe
**Architect in Charge** Qun Wen
**Design Team** Jianning Ma, Gen Li, Jiarui Li, Mingwang Huo, Frank Li, Jing Du, Chen Liu, Kaiqi Yang, Xiaodan Chang, Zhuojun Niu
**Completion Year** 2021
**Built Area** 3,800 m²
**Project Location** Heze, Shandong, China

The project is located in Heze City, Shandong Province, in an undeveloped commercial area. The project will be used as a sales office.

To become a demonstration area for the entire area, the visibility and reachability of the project and its relevance to the construction of commerce have become the focus of design considerations.

The two buildings are separate in the northwest corner of the plot, and the planned smart land on the side, along the cognition of Qiantang Road, we will consider the cognitive volume of the commercial area to be divided into two, connect the bridge block space and form a corridor between the two blocks, leading and guiding into the commercial area.

The architectural space is composed of two parts: virtual and real. The virtual space is enclosed by glass curtain walls, which are visually light and transparent. The solid part uses stone to highlight its heavy sense of volume. The entity occupies the space, defines the space and forms a new environment with the space to form a new

visual product to create a new "space theater."

The virtual and real space blocks are interspersed with each other, opening holes in the façade according to the function, and forming different forms of openings according to the needs of the internal function for lighting, which also makes the façade more changeable. The façade of the physical part is made of Roman travertine, showing the elegant and stable texture of the project. The physical part extends all the way to the interior, emphasizing the interspersion of the blocks, so that the interior and exterior form a whole.

In terms of functional layout, the first and second floors are used as public areas, and the third floor is the office area. The larger volume on the west side is the main sales area. The large sand table is placed in a two-story high-level space and visitors can overlook the entire sand table from the second floor and the bridge. The east side block serves as a commercial display area. The second floor on the west side is set up as a brand display space, which is connected to the financial contract area on the east side through a bridge.

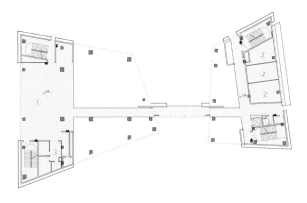

second floor plan

01 display area    02 office area    03 rest room

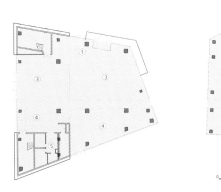

ground floor plan

01 reception    03 model area    05 rest room
02 display area    04 discussion area    06 equipment

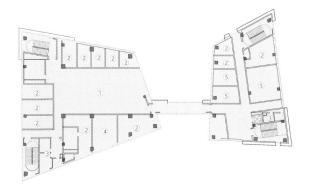

third floor plan

01 work area    03 rest room    05 meeting room
02 office    04 vip room

selected works —— 259

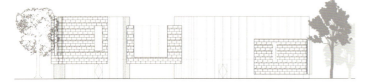
south elevation

260 —— aoe Exploring possibilities: A journey of architectural fantasy

selected works — 261

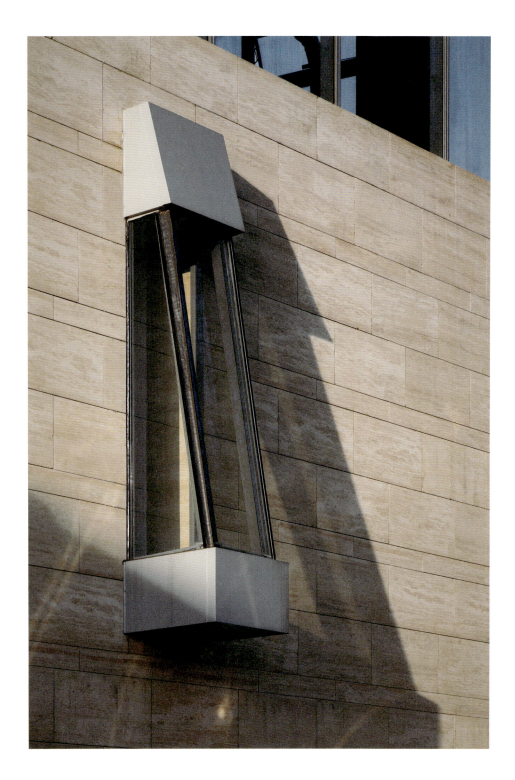

selected works — 263

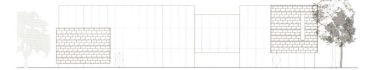

north elevation

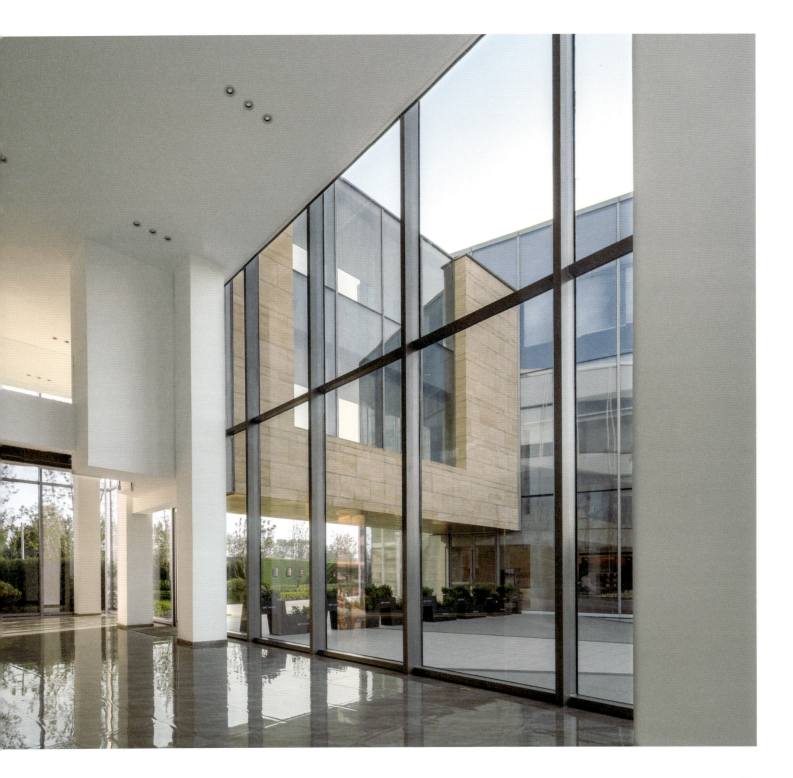

selected works —— 265

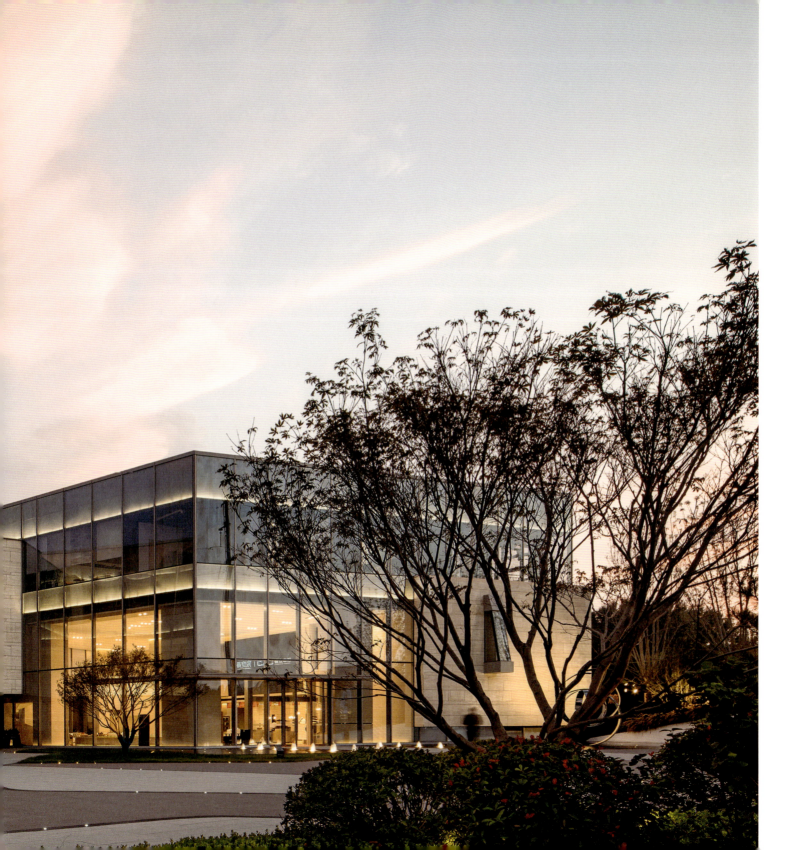

selected works —— 269

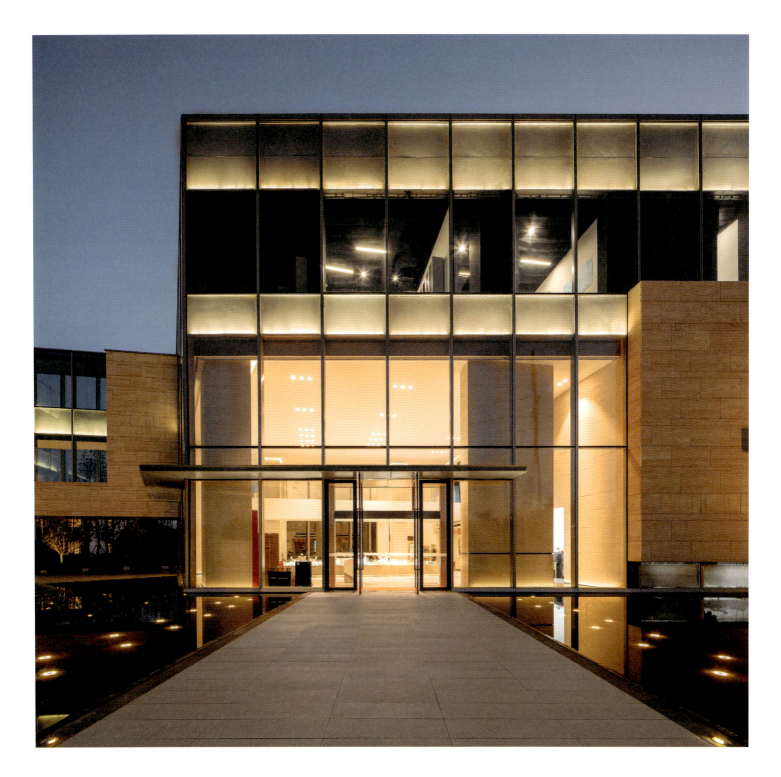

Yongjiang Reception Center

**Project Name** Yongjiang Reception Center
**Architect or Architecture Firm** aoe
**Architect in Charge** Qun Wen
**Technical Director** Jianning Ma
**Design Team** Jian Lu, Jianxin Li, Lu Zhang, Yuqing Lin, Xiao Tang
**Completion Year** 2021
**Built Area** 3,357 m²
**Project Location** Chongqing, China

The project is located in Wanzhou, Chongqing, on the edge of a cliff with a vertical height of about 30 meters close to the Yangtze River. The unique site provides a unique experience for the project but also brings a lot of challenges to the design. The total construction area of the project is about 3000 square meters that include a landscape elevator connected to the height difference of the cliff, the main building of the experience hall and the view tower to enjoy the river view.

Since the building is located on the top of the cliff how to realize the visibility and accessibility of the building has become a consideration in the design. At the same time, the building needs to be integrated with the overall environment and cannot cause damage to the environment. Therefore, the inspiration of design naturally comes from the mountain. The building volume of the folded surface, the plane division of the folded line and the tortuous and changeable internal path form a spatial relationship that simulates a natural cave with rich volume and variable space.

The main structure of the building is a glass polyhedron. Several discrete glass volumes are formed according to the functions. The columns are completely separated from the glass volumes. The glass polyhedron is covered by a roof supported the stone pillars. The roof also adopts a polyline-shaped architectural vocabulary. A large number of gaps are extruded by the stone pillars and the glass polyhedron under the roof

which becomes a rich gray space in the project. At the same time, the roof of some gray space is excavated. Holes of different sizes are also used in the form of polygons to simulate the shape of natural caves. The sunlight pours down through the holes which enriches the spatial experience of the gray space.

As an important traffic space connecting the height difference of 30 meters, the landscape elevator is relatively more obvious in terms of volume, but at the same time it will appear more abrupt. In order to avoid the abruptness of tall and large volume under the premise of ensuring the obviousness in design we compared multiple schemes, and the final design also adopts the form of polyhedron. The elevator as a whole is more like a stone pillar standing between the mountains; the rest platform at the top of the elevator adopts a relatively exaggerated treatment method, forming a strong sense of conflict. The relationship between the volumes shows the image of the entrance and at the same time forms an excellent viewing point.

In order to better appreciate the river view and the urban landscape of Wanzhou, the design adds the view tower. The view tower protrudes beyond the cliff body and has a wider field of vision. At the same time when entering the view tower, the design through two wall frame defines a landscape and draw on the design techniques of framing and borrowing in garden design to form a different viewing effect.

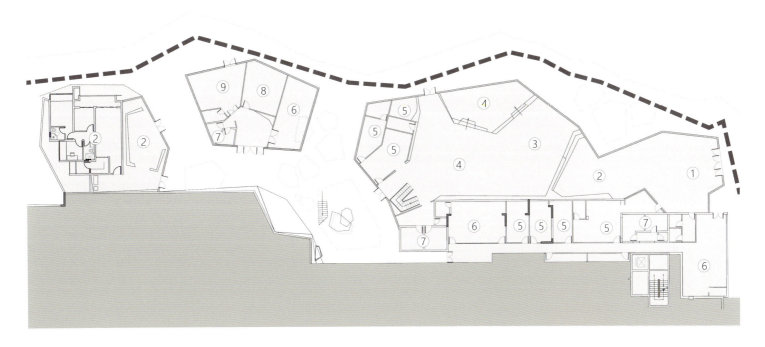

**ground floor plan**

01 foyer
02 display area
03 model area
04 discussion area
05 office
06 meeting room
07 rest room
08 dinning room
09 gym

selected works —— 279

section

selected works

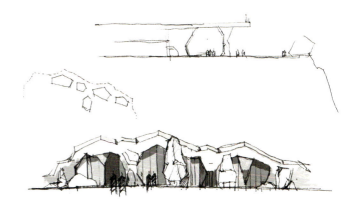

selected works —— 285

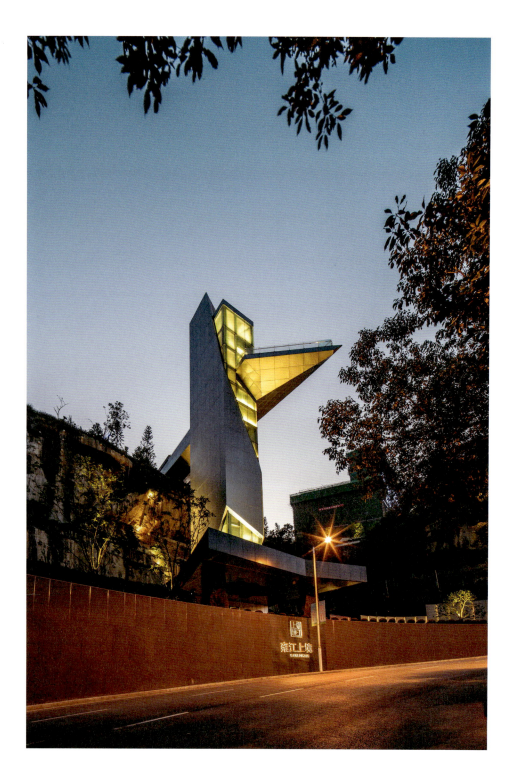

288 ——— aoe  Exploring possibilities: A journey of architectural fantasy

selected works ——— 289

# epilogue

by
Qun Wen

In the middle of 2021, we received an email from Oscar Riera Ojeda Publishers, which said that they were very interested in our ShuiFa Info Town Property Exhibition Center project in Jinan, China, and asked if we would like to produce an book for this project. Such an email makes us very happy because we feel that our project has been paid attention to and recognized. After careful consideration, we decided to use this opportunity to summarize our architectural practice in the past five years and select ten representative projects to express our practical ideas. Then we sent an email to Oscar Riera Ojeda Publishers to express our ideas and got a happy affirmation.

As an architectural design firm with a history of only five years, our practice journey is very difficult, and we have encountered many setbacks in the process. But at the same time, we are also very lucky to get some opportunities to realize our architectural ideas. In these five years, we have designed and completed nearly 20 projects in different scales. Almost every project has won high-level international awards. For a young design company, this is a very proud achievement. It is worthy of every designer who participates in and contributes to these projects.

The ten projects selected in this book represent our exploration and efforts in the past five years. We hope to convey our design concept through this book, and also hope to take this opportunity to make a little contribution to this challenging and wonderful industry and encourage our peers. In the future, we will have a longer road full of hardships and fun, and we will still face all kinds of setbacks and difficulties. As a design company with high-quality design as the core value, we hope to bring our excellent design to our owners, users, communities and cities, and continuously improve our living environment.

Finally, I would like to take this opportunity to thank all the people who have given us support and help in the process of our growth.

Thank you.

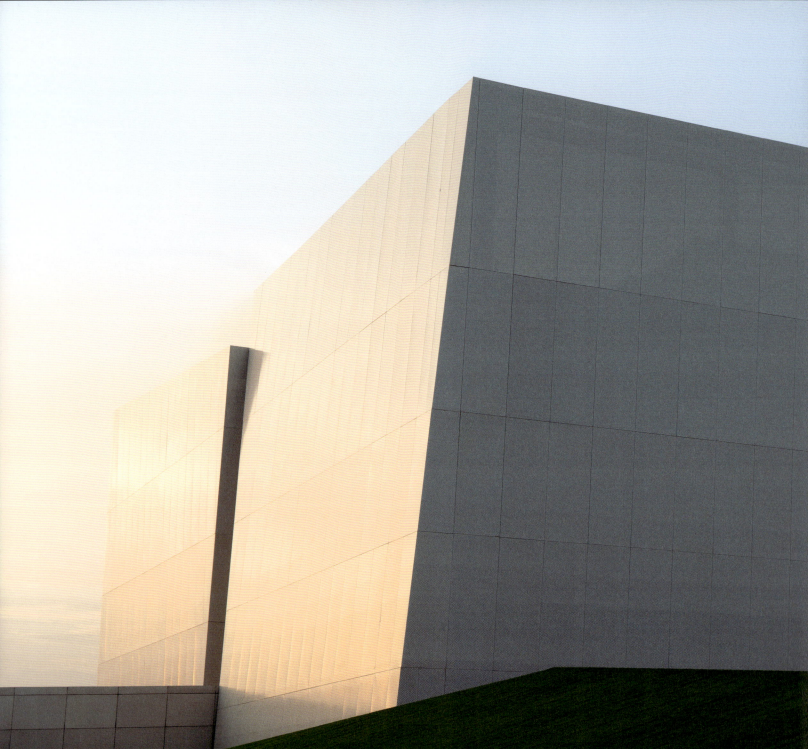

# firm profile

# aoe
# architects

Qun Wen, CEO

aoe is an award-winning Beijing based architectural design practice established in September 2016. The name of aoe (architecture of event) derives from the expression of "there is no architecture without event" by the American architect Bernard Tschumi. The architectural philosophy beyond this statement is the core value of aoe's practice. aoe is a dynamic design force in the fast changing world focusing on the goal to improve the living environment by engaging new technologies, materials, social value, history, art and culture. When designing, aoe studies and refines the vivid relationship between architecture, space and its users to encourage the positive impact on the society with innovative design solutions. The natural logic of being such as space, material, construction and technology is the key driven force to generate the space and form. aoe's solution oriented design approach provides professional services to maximize the success of every project.

aoe team

Jianning Ma, Technical Director; Fanny Fei, CFO; Shixin Gao, Senior Architect; Xiangting Li, Senior Architect; Baoli Ma, Senior Architect; Jichang Pan, Senior Architect; Xiao Tang, Senior Architect; Yue Zhao, Senior Architect; Zhiyu Chang, Architect; Ruixue Fan, Architect; Xiao Hai, Architect; Shawn Li, Architect; Joyce Liu, Architect; Zhiyu Wang, Architect; Sandy Yan, Marketing; Lu Zhang, Architect; Rui Zhang, Architect; Jing Du, Senior Interior Designer; Sha Li, Interior Designer; Meijun Liu, Interior Designer; Changyu Jin, Administration Manager; Zoey Song, Business Manager

# Book Credits

Graphic Design by Lucía B. Bauzá.
Art Direction by Oscar Riera Ojeda.
Copy Editing by Kit Maude & Michael W. Phillips Jr.

**OSCAR RIERA OJEDA**
PUBLISHERS

Copyright © 2022 by Oscar Riera Ojeda Publishers Limited
ISBN 978-1-946226-68-6
Published by Oscar Riera Ojeda Publishers Limited
Printed in China

Oscar Riera Ojeda Publishers Limited
Unit 1003-04, 10/F.,
Shanghai Industrial Investment Building,
48-62 Hennessy Road, Wanchai, Hong Kong

Production Offices
Suit 19, Shenyun Road,
Nanshan District, Shenzhen 518055, China

International Customer Service & Editorial Questions: +1-484-502-5400

www.oropublishers.com | www.oscarrieraojeda.com
oscar@oscarrieraojeda.com

All rights reserved. No part of this book may be reproduced, stored in a retrieval system, or transmitted in any form or by any means, including electronic, mechanical, photocopying of microfilming, recording, or otherwise (except that copying permitted by Sections 107 and 108 of the U.S. Copyright Law and except by reviewers for the public press) without written permission from the publisher.